THE
ARTISANAL
KITCHEN

HOLIDAY
COOKIES

THE ARTISANAL KITCHEN

HOLIDAY COOKIES

The ULTIMATE CHEWY, GOOEY, CRISPY, CRUNCHY TREATS

ALICE MEDRICH

ARTISAN | NEW YORK

CONTENTS

COOKIES

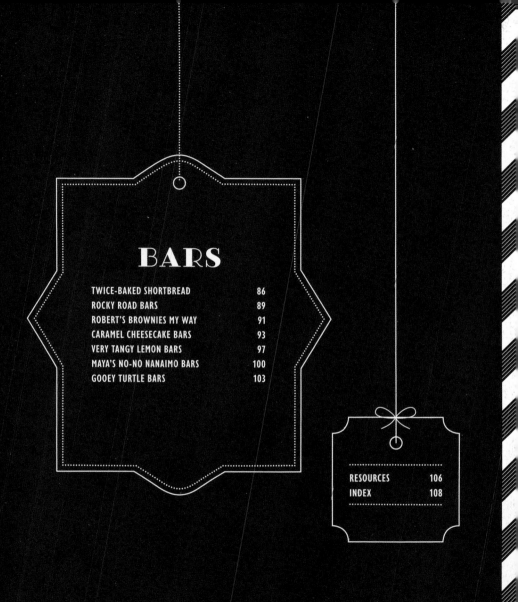

BARS

INTRODUCTION

Cookies are easy, enticing, and fun. They invite creativity and reward experimentation—no rocket science required. An array of cookies is inherently festive—nothing says "holiday" better! Whether you're creating a dessert spread for Thanksgiving, toting a hostess gift to a dinner party, or joining a cookie swap, homemade cookies are *always* in style.

These holiday cookies were handpicked from my repertoire—including familiar favorites and my own inventions—honed over the years to reflect today's spirit of adventure and culinary sensibilities. I selected them by asking myself, "Do I still love these? Do they appeal to our tastes today?" Some have more spice than our moms and grandmas used, or new spices. Some have different leavenings, baking temperatures, or pan liners—to improve textures—than you might be used to. Some have a tad less sugar or butter or more salt to heighten flavors. Some include ingredients that we now adore but which were once considered too exotic or hard to get.

In an era when most people cling to the recipe on the bag of chocolate chips (or buy rather than bake cookies), you will find these recipes updated but still friendly, outrageously good, and even hip (but not too hip!). In the bargain, you'll get my best tips and tricks for making the best cookies of your life.

You'll love the perfect simplicity of crunchy-but-tender butter cookies—nothing more than butter, flour, sugar, vanilla, and salt—and festive variations like Eggnog Cookies and Bourbon Pecan Butter Cookies. Let the fragrance of warm spices and molasses fill your home with holiday spirit; don't miss My Ginger Cookies (made in one bowl and with loads of ginger!) and pretty jam-filled Linzer Cookies. Invited to a cookie swap? A gooey bar or a dramatic cookie—Robert's Brownies My Way, Caramel Cheesecake Bars, Very Tangy Lemon Bars, or Bittersweet Decadence Cookies—will steal the show and burnish your reputation as the best cookie baker ever! Happy holidays to all.

USER'S GUIDE

No matter what kind of cookie you choose, you will get the most from this book if you read the information in this chapter before you start with any of the recipes.

Cookie recipes are the simplest in the baker's repertoire: ingredient lists are brief and familiar, and instructions are few and uncomplicated. But simplicity does not mean a recipe can be executed casually, that the details are whimsical, or that the measurements are flexible. In reality, cookies are tiny pastries. As such, they are subject to all the rules of baking: mundane acts of measuring and mixing, cookie sheet preparation, oven temperature, and timing make the difference between tough and tender cookies and between ordinary and extraordinary cookies. If you've ever eaten ten chocolate chip cookies made by ten different bakers all using the same recipe, you know what I mean.

The information that follows will get you into my kitchen and my head by explaining why I do what I do and why some of my methods may be different from what you are accustomed to or what you find in other books.

DECODING RECIPE LANGUAGE

A good recipe uses specific descriptive language to tell you what to do, when and for how long to do it, and with what utensil. It includes visual cues to look for so you know you are on the right track. All of this is designed to help you achieve results that resemble those that we got in my kitchen. If you change the details, you will change the results—for better or for worse!

Phrases like *just until* are important. When the recipe asks you to mix just until the dry ingredients are blended, or warm the chocolate just until it is melted, or bake just until the edges are brown, you know that more mixing, warming, or baking is not better and your cookies could suffer.

The texture of your cookie is also affected by how you mix: terms like *stir*, *fold*, *beat*, and *whip* are used to guide you. When a recipe calls for mixing, stirring, or folding, you are meant to act gently (but decisively) to incorporate ingredients without destroying or changing the texture of the batter. For beaten egg whites, the goal is to preserve as much of the air in the batter as possible—excessive or vigorous mixing or the wrong stroke will deflate these batters. For denser, richer batters (like those for chocolate chip cookies or butter cookies), excessive or vigorous mixing may add too much air or activate too much gluten.

When a recipe calls for beating, whipping, or mixing vigorously, you are meant to aerate the mixture and/or make sure that the ingredients are emulsified. This is done with an electric mixer or by hand, depending on the recipe. Egg whites are whipped at medium to high speed with an electric mixer with the whisk attachment. Heavier, richer batters and doughs are mixed with the flat beater or paddle attachment or by hand with a spatula at a brisk pace.

Finally, note that measures given in ounces always refer to weights rather than volume (see page 12 for a fuller explanation).

FAQS

Successful baking is all in the details. The simplest things can make the difference between a perfectly tender cookie and a doughy paperweight, between a soggy cookie and one that is sublimely crisp. Each recipe spells out the important details for that cookie, but here is the background.

What makes cookies tough?

Tough cookies often result from badly measured flour, the wrong kind of flour (bread flour or whole-grain flours rather than all-purpose flour), too much mixing after the flour has been added to the moist ingredients in the batter, or too much flour used to keep the dough from sticking to the rolling pin or the countertop. Other culprits include too much kneading and rerolling of scraps and baking at too high or too low a temperature or for too long.

The fix? Use the flour called for in the recipe, measure it accurately, mix it just enough (as called for in the recipe), avoid excessive rerolling, roll out between sheets of wax paper or plastic wrap, and check your oven and timer. You may also increase tenderness with a finer granulation of sugar, either by using superfine sugar or by grinding regular sugar to a finer consistency in a food processor.

How important is careful measuring?

A creative approach to measuring does not always spoil cookies. You may use a liberal hand with raisins, nuts, chocolate chips, coconut, or even vanilla. Feel free to substitute dried fruits and nuts one for another and to experiment with extracts and flavors.

But for cookies with great textures, and to avoid dry, tough, and leaden cookies, you must carefully measure the baking soda, baking powder, salt, and, most of all, flour. I cannot emphasize enough how many cookie problems can be prevented by knowing how to measure flour correctly.

Is it better to measure with a scale?

A cup of flour can weigh anywhere from 4 ounces to well over 6 ounces, depending on a number of factors, including whether the flour was compacted, loosened, or sifted; whether the measuring cup was dipped into the flour or the flour was spooned lightly into the cup; and, finally, whether the measure was leveled by tapping or shaking the cup or simply by sweeping a knife across the rim. Given so many variables, your results will be more consistent from batch to batch and closer to the results that I got in my kitchen if you weigh most ingredients—not just flour—instead of using measuring cups. Weighing is also faster and produces fewer dirty dishes than measuring with cups.

If I don't have a scale, how should I measure flour with cups?

For 1 cup of flour, measure the flour (without sifting* it) using a 1-cup dry measure as follows: Gently loosen the flour in the sack or canister with a spoon, but avoid excessive stirring or whisking or your cup of flour will be too light. Spoon the flour lightly into the measure, without packing it, until it is heaped above the rim. Don't shake or tap the cup. Sweep a straight-edged knife or spatula or your finger across the rim of the cup to level the measure. Your level cup should weigh about 4½ ounces.

What are dry and liquid measures, and how are they used?

Dry measures refer to measuring cups designed to measure dry ingredients; these are meant to be filled to the rim and leveled as described above. When

---

*Ignore the "pre-sifted" label on flour sacks. Pre-sifting eliminates stones and foreign matter, but it cannot prevent the flour from compacting again en route to your grocer's shelf.

using dry measures, use a 1-cup measure to measure 1 cup, a ½-cup measure to measure ½ cup, and so forth.

Liquid measures are designed to measure liquid ingredients. These are clear plastic or glass pitchers marked with measurements on the sides. To measure, set the measure on the counter—no one can hold a cup level in the air. Pour liquid up to the appropriate mark with your head lowered to read the measurement at eye level.

Can I use the ounces printed on my liquid measuring cup instead of a scale?

Alas, no. The ounces printed on the sides of glass measures are fluid ounces for measuring volume, not weight. One cup of anything is always 8 fluid ounces, but 8 fluid ounces of raisins does not weigh the same as 8 fluid ounces of honey or 8 fluid ounces of cornflakes. In my recipes, ounces refer to weight unless otherwise noted.

How soft is softened butter?

If the recipe calls for softened butter and you are mixing with an electric mixer, allow the butter to soften at room temperature (or in the microwave at 30 percent power for a few seconds at a time) until it is pliable but not completely squishy, 65° to 70°F. If you are mixing with a large spoon or a rubber spatula, soften butter to the consistency of mayonnaise, 75° to 80°F.

What's the best way to melt chocolate?

Unsweetened, bittersweet, or semisweet chocolate should be coarsely chopped before melting. White and milk chocolate should be finely chopped.

If you are melting chocolate by itself, with nothing else added to it, the goal is to heat the chocolate gently until it is warm (not hot) and perfectly fluid.

To this end, the cutting board, bowl, and all utensils should be dry, as small amounts of moisture or liquid may cause the chocolate to thicken or seize instead of melting smoothly.

While most cookbooks advise using a double boiler or a microwave for melting chocolate, I find it both safe and flexible to use an open water bath—a wide skillet of hot (see Note below for white or milk chocolate), not even simmering water with a heatproof (preferably stainless-steel) bowl of chocolate set directly into it. It is easy to keep an eye on the water and turn the heat down or off if the water begins to boil, easy to watch and stir the chocolate as it melts, and easy to use a bowl that is the right size for the quantity of chocolate or the recipe. Should you prefer to use the classic double boiler instead, it is perfectly okay if the upper container touches the water below. The key to not burning chocolate has more to do with paying attention to the temperature of the chocolate and the water than whether or not the bowl touches the water! With either method, stir the chocolate frequently, dip a finger in now and then to gauge the temperature, and remove the bowl when the chocolate is melted or almost melted. Easy!

Note: To melt white or milk chocolate (both of which are more heat sensitive than dark chocolate), bring the skillet of water to a simmer, then remove it from the burner and wait 60 seconds before setting the bowl of chocolate into it and stir frequently; the hot water will do the job safely without live heat under the pan.

How do I toast coconut?
Have a medium bowl ready near the stove. Spread the coconut in a wide heavy skillet over medium heat. Stir constantly until the coconut begins to color slightly. Turn the heat down (once hot, coconut burns quickly) and continue to stir until the coconut bits are mostly light golden brown flecked with some white. I often take the pan off the heat early and continue to stir, letting the residual heat of the pan finish toasting the coconut slowly and

evenly. The whole process takes less than 5 minutes. Immediately scrape the coconut into the bowl.

How do I toast nuts?

To toast nuts, spread them in a single layer on an ungreased cookie sheet. Bake in a preheated oven (350°F for almonds and hazelnuts; 325°F for pecans and walnuts) for 10 to 20 minutes, depending on the type of nut and whether they are whole, sliced, or slivered. Check the color and flavor of the nuts frequently and stir to redistribute them on the pan. When chopped toasted nuts are called for, toast them whole or in large pieces, then chop them. Almonds and hazelnuts are done when they are golden brown when you bite or cut them in half. To rub the skins from toasted hazelnuts, cool them thoroughly, then rub them together in your hands or in a tea towel or place them in a large coarse-mesh strainer and rub them against the mesh until most of the skins flake off. Pecans and walnuts are done when fragrant and lightly colored.

How do I grind nuts?

To pulverize or grind nuts in a food processor without making paste or nut butter, start with a perfectly dry processor bowl and blade at room tempera-ture (not hot from the dishwasher) and nuts at room temperature. (Frozen or cold nuts will produce moisture that turns the nuts to paste, as will nuts still hot from the oven.) Use short pulses, stopping from time to time to scrape the sides of the processor bowl with a skewer or chopstick. If you observe these rules, there is no particular need to add flour or sugar from the recipe to the nuts to keep them dry, although that is a good precaution.

How important is mixing technique?

Cookie flavor and texture are a function of the type and amount of ingredients in the recipe. But mixing time and technique have a surprisingly significant effect as well.

There are two critical stages of mixing. Most recipes begin with mixing the butter with sugar. The consistency of the butter and how long and vigorously it is beaten with the sugar affect the texture and the intensity of the flavor in subtle yet wonderful ways. I find that shortbread and chocolate chip cookies are best when the butter is melted completely and simply stirred with the sugar. Butter cookies have a superior flavor and texture when the butter is just softened and beaten, by hand or with an electric mixer, but only until smooth and creamy. Sugar cookies are at their best when pliable butter is beaten with sugar with an electric mixer until light and fluffy.

Flour is normally added at the end of the recipe. This is the second critical mixing phase for most cookie recipes. How long and vigorously the flour is mixed into the dough has an important—and not at all subtle—effect on cookies! Once flour is added to the moist ingredients, excessive mixing makes tough cookies. The goal then is to blend the flour thoroughly into the dough or batter with as little mixing as possible. The trick is to be sure that the flour is first mixed thoroughly with other dry ingredients (especially leavening and sometimes spices and salt) and that it is aerated and fluffed up rather than compacted and clumped, so that it will blend easily into the dough. Toward this end, I mix dry ingredients together with a wire whisk, which aerates at the same time as it mixes.

To add the flour without excessive mixing, I like to turn off the mixer (if I am using one) and add all the flour mixture at one time and then commence mixing at low speed. Otherwise, add the dry ingredients gradually enough to avoid flying flour but without taking any more time than necessary. Or mix in the flour with a spoon or your hands. In any case, mix only long enough to blend in the flour.

If the dough is relatively stiff, as with butter or sugar cookies, scrape the dough into a mass and knead it with your hands a few times just until smooth and with any traces of dry flour incorporated.

Why chill and rest cookie dough?

Cookies are so simple to make that it seems a shame to deny the convenience, and the instant gratification, of mixing and baking on the spur of the moment.

In the case of slice-and-bake or roll-and-cut cookies, chilling makes the slicing, rolling, and cutting possible. But even cookies spooned and dropped right onto the pan may be improved with chilling/resting. Gluten developed in mixing or rolling out dough is relaxed while the dough rests, so cookies become more tender. Moisture in the dough is absorbed by the dry ingredients and dissolves some of the sugar. This causes extra caramelization (browning), which improves flavor. Flavors become more developed and better integrated when dough has rested, and some cookies end up both more tender and crisper. Although wheat-free or gluten-free cookies that are made with nonwheat flours don't have the same gluten or toughness problem, resting benefits these doughs as well. I've found that letting dough with nonwheat flours and starches rest and absorb moisture causes the starches to gelatinize and cook more thoroughly, and this eliminates the unpleasant raw starch flavor that plagues many gluten-free treats. For me this was a trial-and-error discovery that made my experiments turn out much better.

If chilled cookie dough is too stiff to scoop, let it soften at room temperature. A chilled log of dough may need to soften briefly at room temperature as well.

Can I cheat on the chilling time?

When the recipe says, "If possible, chill the dough . . . ," then cheat if you must. Your cookies will still be tasty and delicious. But compare cookies mixed and baked immediately with cookies baked after an overnight chill and you may change your cookie-making habits forever.

Can cookie dough be frozen?

As a rule, most stiff doughs (as opposed to wetter batters and meringues, etc.) can be frozen—and for at least 3 months, before they deteriorate in quality.

The quality of the cookies baked from frozen dough depends on how well you wrap the dough and whether your freezer actually keeps things frozen.

For slice-and-bake cookies, freeze cookie dough after shaping it into logs rolled up in parchment or wax paper. Wrap the logs again in heavy-duty foil. Then put them into an airtight freezer bag or a sealed freezer container.

For roll-and-cut cookies, form patties as directed in the recipe and wrap them in plastic wrap. Wrap again in foil and then put them into a freezer bag or a sealed freezer container.

For drop cookies (chocolate chip, gingersnaps), freeze the whole mass in a freezer bag and then put that into another freezer bag or a sealed container; or you can shape the dough into cookie-size portions by freezing them on a cookie sheet, then double-bagging them in freezer bags.

What is the best way to roll and cut cookies?

Traditionally, cookie dough is rolled out on a well-floured board with a floured rolling pin and lots of flour sprinkled everywhere to prevent it from sticking. All that excess flour tends to toughen the cookies, and the procedure is tricky for inexperienced bakers anyway.

A better, easier, and less messy technique is to roll the dough between sheets of wax paper, plastic wrap, or a cut-apart heavy resealable plastic bag.

Cookie dough softens quickly once it comes out of the refrigerator. If you have more than one patty of dough to roll out, remove them one at a time, a few minutes apart, so they won't be too soft to work with when you get to them.

Let the dough sit at room temperature until it is supple enough to roll but still quite firm. It will continue to soften as you work. Roll the dough to the required thickness between the sheets of wax paper or plastic wrap or the cut-apart plastic bag. Roll from the center up to, but never over, the edge of the dough, rotating the dough as you work. Turn over the dough and attached sheets now and then to check for deep wrinkles. If necessary, peel off and smooth a wrinkled sheet over the dough before continuing to roll it. When the dough is thin enough, slide the whole assembly onto a tray and refrigerate it while you roll out the remaining pieces of dough.

To cut out cookies, remove the first piece of dough from the fridge, peel off the top sheet, and place it on the counter in front of you. Flip the dough, still attached to the other sheet, over onto the loose sheet and peel off the attached sheet. Cut shapes close together to minimize scraps, dipping the edges of your cookie cutters in flour as necessary to prevent sticking. Use the point of a paring knife to remove scraps between cookies.

If the dough gets too soft at any time—while you're rolling, removing paper or plastic, cutting, removing scraps between cookies, or transferring cookies— slide a cookie sheet underneath the bottom sheet of paper or plastic and refrigerate the dough for a few minutes, until firm. Repeat with the remaining pieces of dough. Gently press all of the accumulated dough scraps together (don't overwork them with too much kneading) and reroll.

What is the best way to prepare cookie sheets?
My recipes offer options for pan preparation in order of preference, weighing quality of outcome with convenience for the baker.

Pan liners are convenient because they rarely need greasing, they can be pre-loaded while cookie sheets are still in the oven, and you can slide them off the pan and onto racks for cooling (or even set the lined pan itself on a rack to cool), rather than remove hot cookies one by one from hot pans.

Parchment paper is probably the best all-purpose pan liner. Cookies don't stick to it, and its slight insulating effect promotes even baking, prevents chocolaty batters and meringues from scorching, and generally mitigates the effects of poor-quality baking sheets, which might be too dark or too thin. That being said, parchment is not always the first choice. A few cookies (for example, certain chocolate chip cookies) are noticeably more crusty and caramelized around the edges—in contrast to their chewy centers—if baked directly on the pan.

To get the advantages (browning, caramelized flavor, and contrast of texture) of baking directly on the pan as well as the convenience of a liner, you can use foil. Placed dull side up, foil conducts heat and produces results similar to those achieved in an unlined pan. Use regular-weight foil unless heavy-duty foil is called for. Recipes call for the dull side to be up only when it makes a significant difference in results.

Silicone liners or mats (such as Silpat) are especially convenient for very thin, fragile cookies, but they provide too much insulation to be good all-purpose liners.

When it is necessary to grease pans or liners, use a brush or a wad of paper towel to coat them lightly, but thoroughly, with flavorless vegetable oil or melted butter.

What is the best way to line baking pans?
Why line baking pans? It is easier to line pans than to grease them, and lined pans make the removal of bars or brownies easier too.

You can simply line the pan across the bottom and all the way up two opposite sides with foil or parchment.

But a second method (which I prefer) is to line the bottom and all four sides of the pan. Use a sheet of foil or parchment 4 inches wider and longer than the bottom of the pan. Turn the pan upside down and center the liner on it with

2 inches extending on all sides. Fold the excess over the sides of the pan. Fold and crease the corners over as though wrapping a present. Slip the liner off the pan. Turn the pan right side up and insert the liner. To remove brownies or bars from the pan, simply lift the edges of the foil or parchment.

Do I have to preheat the oven?

Oven temperature affects the texture and flavor of cookies as well as the baking time. Cookie dough put into an oven that is not hot enough may spread too much, dry out, or toughen. And different kinds of dough do better at different temperatures. All things considered, you will get better results if cookies go into an oven that is already heated to the optimal temperature. It takes most ovens about 15 minutes to reach a set temperature.

Where should the racks be placed in the oven?

Bake in the center of the oven if you are baking one sheet of cookies at a time, or in the lower third for one pan of brownies or bars. When baking two sheets at a time, position the racks in the upper and lower thirds of the oven, reversing the cookie sheets from upper to lower and from front to back about halfway through the baking period so that the cookies bake evenly.

In a convection oven, you will be able to bake more than two trays at a time and may not have to rotate them if the oven bakes evenly.

Why rotate the pans while baking?

Even if you are baking one sheet of cookies at a time in the center of the oven, chances are your oven is hotter in the back than in the front (if not also different from one side to the other!). Turning the pan around halfway through the baking time produces cookies that are baked about the same regardless of where they were in the oven.

What is the best way to cool cookies?

If you bake on parchment- or foil-lined pans, slide the liner from the hot cookie sheet onto a cooling rack, leaving the cookies attached. Or, if you have enough pans and racks, do what the professionals do: set the hot cookie sheet itself on the rack and allow the cookies to cool on the lined pan. However, if your cookies seem slightly overbaked or verging on overbaked (no one is perfect), slide the liners off immediately rather than let the cookies cool on the pan. Every second counts.

If baking directly on the pan, use a thin, flexible metal pancake turner to transfer each cookie from the pan to cooling racks. Some cookies can be transferred from the pan immediately; others require 1 to 2 minutes of cooling before they are firm or sturdy enough to move without breaking. If the first cookie you transfer breaks or bends, wait a minute or so and try again.

How should cookies be stored and for how long?

Cool cookies thoroughly before stacking or storing in a closed container. Otherwise, they will become soggy (even moldy!) or misshapen from trapped steam.

Most cookies should be stored in airtight containers: tins, jars, resealable plastic bags, or cookie jars with tight-fitting lids. Certain cookies (such as those that are crunchy on the outside and moist within) should be stored in loosely covered containers that allow some air to get in. Different kinds and flavors of cookies should be stored separately or they will all taste pretty much the same and have the same texture after a day or two. Fragile cookies should be stored in wide containers where they can lie flat with parchment or wax paper between layers. If you have iced or decorated your cookies, make sure the decoration is completely dry before layering the cookies between sheets of wax paper.

Unless indicated otherwise, the cookies and bars in this book may be frozen for at least 2 or 3 months.

BASIC BUTTER COOKIES

MAKES ABOUT FORTY-EIGHT 2-INCH COOKIES

Magnificently plain, tender, crunchy cookies celebrate the taste of butter without being too rich or greasy. These are my go-to cookies for holiday decorating—bring on the icing or pure melted chocolate for piping and set out the silver shot, colorful sugar, sprinkles, and more.

INGREDIENTS

14 TABLESPOONS (1¾ STICKS) UNSALTED BUTTER, SOFTENED

¾ CUP (5.25 OUNCES) SUGAR

¼ TEASPOON SALT

1½ TEASPOONS PURE VANILLA EXTRACT

1 LARGE EGG YOLK (OPTIONAL)

2 CUPS (9 OUNCES) UNBLEACHED ALL-PURPOSE FLOUR

EQUIPMENT

COOKIE SHEETS, UNGREASED OR LINED WITH FOIL, DULL SIDE UP

2-INCH COOKIE CUTTER, ROUND OR OTHER SHAPE (OPTIONAL)

HANDHELD MIXER OR STAND MIXER WITH PADDLE ATTACHMENT

With the back of a large spoon or with a handheld mixer in a medium mixing bowl or in the bowl of a stand mixer fitted with the paddle attachment, beat the butter with the sugar, salt, and vanilla until smooth and creamy but not fluffy, about 1 minute with the mixer. Beat in the egg yolk, if using. Add the flour and mix just until incorporated. Scrape the dough into a mass and knead it with your hands a few times just to be sure the flour is completely incorporated.

For slice-and-bake cookies, form a 12-by-2-inch log. For roll-and-cut cookies, form 2 flat patties. Wrap and refrigerate the dough for at least 2 hours and preferably overnight. The dough may be frozen for up to 3 months.

continued

Preheat the oven to 350°F (or 325°F if using the egg yolk). Position racks in the upper and lower thirds of the oven.

To slice and bake cookies: Use a sharp knife to cut the cold dough log into slices ¼ inch thick. Place cookies at least 1½ inches apart on the ungreased or lined cookie sheets.

To roll and cut cookies: Remove 1 patty from the refrigerator and let it sit at room temperature until supple enough to roll but still quite firm, about 20 minutes. It will continue to soften as you work. Roll the dough to a thickness of ¼ inch between two sheets of wax paper or between heavy plastic sheets cut from a resealable plastic bag. Turn the dough over once or twice while you are rolling it out to check for deep wrinkles; if necessary, peel off and smooth the paper or plastic over the dough before continuing to roll it. When the dough is thin enough, peel off the top sheet of paper or plastic and keep it in front of you. Invert the dough onto that sheet and peel off the second sheet. Cut cookie shapes as close together as possible

to minimize scraps, dipping the edges of the cookie cutters in flour as necessary to prevent sticking. Use the point of a paring knife to lift and remove scraps as you transfer cookies to cookie sheets. Place the cookies at least 1½ inches apart on the ungreased or lined cookie sheets. If the dough gets too soft at any time—while you are rolling, cutting, removing scraps between cookies, or transferring cookies—slide a cookie sheet underneath the paper or plastic and refrigerate the dough for a few minutes, until firm. Repeat with the second patty of dough. Gently press all of the dough scraps together (don't overwork them with too much kneading) and reroll.

Bake for 12 to 14 minutes (a bit longer if using the egg yolk dough) or until light golden brown at the edges. Rotate the cookie sheets from top to bottom and from front to back halfway through the baking time to ensure even baking. Repeat until all the cookies are baked.

For lined pans, set the pans or just the liners on racks to cool. For unlined pans, let the cookies firm up on the pans for about 1 minute, then

THE ARTISANAL KITCHEN: *Holiday Cookies*

transfer them to a rack with a metal spatula. Cool completely before stacking or storing. The cookies are delicious fresh but even better the next day. They may be kept in an airtight container for at least 1 month.

....

Bourbon Pecan Butter Cookies: Add 1 tablespoon plus 1 teaspoon bourbon with the vanilla extract. Mix in 1 cup (4 ounces) chopped toasted pecans (see page 14) before adding the flour.

Eggnog Cookies: Use the egg yolk dough and add 1 tablespoon plus 1 teaspoon rum or brandy and ¼ teaspoon freshly grated nutmeg with the vanilla.

ULTRATHIN CHOCOLATE CHUNK COOKIES

A theatrical departure from mainstream chocolate chip cookies, these are large and decidedly flat. They shatter dramatically when you bite into it, releasing loads of caramel brown sugar flavor and bursts of bittersweet chocolate.

INGREDIENTS

1⅓ CUPS (6 OUNCES) UNBLEACHED ALL-PURPOSE FLOUR

½ TEASPOON BAKING SODA

10 TABLESPOONS (1¼ STICKS) UNSALTED BUTTER, MELTED

½ CUP (1.5 OUNCES) QUICK ROLLED OATS

½ CUP (3.5 OUNCES) GRANULATED SUGAR

¼ CUP (1.75 OUNCES) PACKED DARK BROWN SUGAR

2 TABLESPOONS PLUS 1 TEASPOON (2 OUNCES) LIGHT CORN SYRUP

2 TABLESPOONS WHOLE MILK

½ TEASPOON SALT

7 OUNCES BITTERSWEET OR SEMISWEET CHOCOLATE, CHOPPED INTO CHUNKS, OR 1 GENEROUS CUP CHOCOLATE CHIPS OR CHUNKS

EQUIPMENT

COOKIE SHEETS, LINED WITH FOIL, DULL SIDE UP

Preheat the oven to 325°F. Position racks in the upper and lower thirds of the oven.

Combine the flour and baking soda in a small bowl and mix together thoroughly with a whisk or fork.

In a large bowl, whisk together the melted butter, oats, sugars, corn syrup, milk, and salt. Mix in the flour mixture. If the batter is warm from the butter, let it cool before adding the chocolate. Stir in the chocolate chunks. If possible, let the dough

rest for at least several hours at room temperature or (better still) overnight in the fridge. The rest makes for an especially crisp and extra-flavorful cookie!

Divide the dough into 15 equal pieces (each a scant ¼ cup or about 1.75 ounces). Lay out three sheets of aluminum foil, cut to fit your cookie sheets, on the counter. Arrange 5 pieces of dough (4 in a square and 1 in the center) well apart on each sheet of foil, remembering that the cookies will spread to 5 inches. Flatten each piece of dough until it is about 3½ inches in diameter. Slide two of the sheets onto baking sheets.

Bake for 20 to 25 minutes, until the cookies are thin and very brown. If they are too pale, they will not be crisp. Rotate the pans from top to bottom and front to back halfway through the baking time to ensure even baking. Slide the foil with cookies onto racks to cool completely before removing the cookies from the foil. Repeat with the third batch—you can even slide the next foil and cookie dough onto a hot baking sheet as long as you put the pan in the oven immediately. Cool the cookies completely before stacking or storing. They may be kept in an airtight container for at least 3 days.

GREAT GRAHAMS

Real (homemade) grahams are normally hearty and healthy and delicious. A little oat flour softens that mildly bitter whole wheat edge by adding a compelling nuance of sweet oat flavor and an extra-tender crunch. The result is an extra-good graham that is still 100 percent whole grain.

INGREDIENTS

1¾ CUPS (8 OUNCES) GRAHAM FLOUR

½ CUP PLUS 1 TABLESPOON
(2 OUNCES) OAT FLOUR

¼ CUP (1.75 OUNCES) SUGAR,
PLUS EXTRA FOR SPRINKLING

½ TEASPOON SALT

½ TEASPOON BAKING POWDER

¼ TEASPOON BAKING SODA

6 TABLESPOONS COLD UNSALTED
BUTTER, CUT INTO ½-INCH CUBES

3 TABLESPOONS MILK

3 TABLESPOONS HONEY

½ TEASPOON PURE VANILLA EXTRACT

EQUIPMENT

COOKIE SHEET

2 SHEETS OF PARCHMENT PAPER
CUT TO FIT THE PAN

FOOD PROCESSOR

In a food processor, combine the flours, the ¼ cup sugar, the salt, baking powder, and baking soda. Pulse to mix thoroughly. Sprinkle the butter cubes over the flour mixture. Pulse until the mixture resembles cornmeal. In a small cup, stir the milk, honey, and vanilla together until the honey is dissolved. Drizzle the honey mixture into the bowl. Process just until the mixture gathers into a single mass.

Shape the dough into a flat 8- or 9-inch-square patty. Wrap and refrigerate it until very firm but supple enough to roll out, 20 to 30 minutes. Or keep it refrigerated for up to 2 days and then let soften slightly at room temperature before rolling.

continued

Preheat the oven to 350°F. Position a rack in the center of the oven.

Roll the dough between the sheets of parchment paper until it is about ⅛ inch thick and as even as possible from the center to the edges. Flip the paper and dough over once or twice to check for deep wrinkles; if necessary, peel off the parchment and smooth it over the dough before continuing. Peel off the top sheet of parchment. Sprinkle the dough evenly with 2 to 3 teaspoons sugar. Prick the dough all over with a fork. Slide the parchment with dough attached onto the pan. With a sharp knife, even up the edges of the dough and score it into squares or rectangles. Leave edge scraps in place (for nibbling and to protect the rest of the grahams from burnt edges).

Bake for 20 to 25 minutes, until the grahams are golden brown with deep brown edges. Rotate the pan from front to back halfway through the baking time to ensure even baking. Set the pan on a rack to cool. Break the grahams along the score lines. Cool the grahams completely before storing. They may be kept in an airtight container for at least 3 weeks.

NOTE

Checking Grahams for Crunch
Grahams crisp up after they are completely cool unless they are underbaked. If your grahams are not thoroughly crunchy when cool (especially the ones in the center, which might be a little thicker), return them (on a parchment-lined baking sheet) to a preheated 325°F oven for 10 to 15 minutes. Let cool and check for crunch.

UPGRADES
....

Ginger Oat Grahams: Add a slightly rounded tablespoon of ground ginger to the processor with the flour.

Spicy Oat Grahams: Add 1 teaspoon ground cinnamon, 2 teaspoons ground ginger, ½ teaspoon ground cloves, and ¼ teaspoon ground cardamom to the processor with the flour.

CHUNKY HAZELNUT MERINGUES

Light, sweet, and tenderly crunchy cookies with hidden pockets of dark chocolate and toasty nuts. Serve them with blackberries and unsweetened whipped cream. Of course you can substitute toasted almonds—or any other nut you like—for the hazelnuts.

INGREDIENTS

5 OUNCES BITTERSWEET OR SEMISWEET CHOCOLATE, CHOPPED, OR 1 SCANT CUP CHOCOLATE CHUNKS OR CHIPS

1 CUP (5 OUNCES) TOASTED AND SKINNED HAZELNUTS (SEE PAGE 14), COARSELY CHOPPED

3 LARGE EGG WHITES, AT ROOM TEMPERATURE

⅛ TEASPOON CREAM OF TARTAR

⅔ CUP (4.625 OUNCES) SUGAR

CINNAMON STICK (OPTIONAL)

EQUIPMENT

COOKIE SHEETS, LINED WITH PARCHMENT PAPER

STAND MIXER WITH WHISK ATTACHMENT OR HANDHELD MIXER

Preheat the oven to 300°F. Position racks in the upper and lower thirds of the oven.

Set aside about one-fifth of the chocolate and the nuts for topping the cookies.

Combine the egg whites and cream of tartar in a clean dry mixer bowl. Beat on medium-high speed with a stand mixer fitted with the whisk attachment (or on high speed with a handheld mixer) until the egg whites are creamy white (instead of translucent) and hold a soft shape when the beaters are lifted. Continue to beat on medium-high speed, adding the sugar a little at a time, taking 1½ to 2 minutes in all.

continued

The mixture should stand in very stiff peaks when the beaters are lifted. Use a rubber spatula to fold in the chocolate and nuts just until incorporated.

Drop heaping teaspoons of meringue 1½ inches apart on the lined cookie sheets. Top each meringue with some of the reserved chocolate and nuts. Bake for 10 to 15 minutes, until the meringues begin to turn golden. Rotate the pans from top to bottom and from front to back. Turn the oven down to 200°F and bake for another 1½ hours. Turn off the oven and leave the meringues in it to cool. Let the cookies cool completely before using or storing. If desired, grate a little of the cinnamon stick over each cookie before serving. The cookies may be kept in an airtight container for at least 2 months.

UPGRADE

....

Mocha-Nut Meringue Kisses: Combine 1½ teaspoons instant espresso powder with the sugar before adding it to the egg whites. Skip the 10-to-15-minute bake at 300°F. Bake for 2 hours at 200°F and rotate the pans from top to bottom and from front to back after 1 hour.

BITTERSWEET DECADENCE COOKIES

MAKES 30 TO 36 COOKIES

Richer than sin, with an irresistible jolt of unrelenting bittersweet chocolate, these cookies are slightly crunchy on the outside with chunky but divinely gooey centers. For the best gooey texture and balanced flavor, pay attention to the amount of chocolate vis-à-vis the specific cacao percentages called for in the first part of the ingredient list and the sugar adjustment. For the chocolate chunks, I like to chop my own from a bar of bittersweet with 70% or up to 82% cacao for a deeply dramatic contrast to the flavor and sweetness of the batter. This ultrachocolaty batter begins to stiffen almost as soon as you mix it. Your cookies will look best if you scoop them ASAP, while the batter is still soft.

INGREDIENTS

¼ CUP (1.125 OUNCES) UNBLEACHED ALL-PURPOSE FLOUR

¼ TEASPOON BAKING POWDER

⅛ TEASPOON SALT

8 OUNCES BITTERSWEET OR SEMISWEET CHOCOLATE WITH UP TO 60% CACAO OR 7 OUNCES CHOCOLATE WITH 61% TO 64% CACAO, CHOPPED

2 TABLESPOONS UNSALTED BUTTER

2 LARGE EGGS

½ CUP (3.5 OUNCES) SUGAR (PLUS 1 TABLESPOON [0.375 OUNCE] IF USING CHOCOLATE WITH 61% TO 64% CACAO)

1 TEASPOON PURE VANILLA EXTRACT

6 OUNCES SEMISWEET OR BITTERSWEET CHOCOLATE WITH ANY PERCENTAGE CACAO YOU LIKE, CHOPPED INTO GENEROUS-SIZE CHUNKS, OR PURCHASED CHOCOLATE CHUNKS

2 CUPS (7 OUNCES) WALNUT OR PECAN HALVES OR LARGE PIECES

EQUIPMENT

COOKIE SHEETS, LINED WITH PARCHMENT PAPER

continued

Preheat the oven to 350°F. Position racks in the upper and lower thirds of the oven.

Combine the flour, baking powder, and salt in a small bowl and mix together thoroughly with a whisk.

Place the 8 ounces chocolate and the butter in a large heatproof bowl set directly in a wide skillet of barely simmering water. Stir frequently just until melted and smooth. Remove the chocolate from the skillet and set it aside. Leave the heat on under the skillet.

In another large heatproof bowl, whisk the eggs, sugar, and vanilla together thoroughly. Set the bowl in the skillet and stir until the mixture is lukewarm to the touch. Stir the egg mixture into the warm (not hot) chocolate. Stir in the flour mixture, then the chocolate chunks and nuts.

Scoop slightly rounded tablespoons of batter and place 1½ inches apart on the lined cookie sheets. Bake for 12 to 14 minutes, until the surface

of the cookie looks dry and set and the centers are still gooey. Rotate the sheets from top to bottom and from front to back halfway through the baking time to ensure even baking. Set the pans or just the liners on racks to cool.

Let the cookies cool completely before storing or stacking. They may be kept in an airtight container for up to 3 days.

NOTE
To Make the Dough Ahead
Refrigerate or freeze scoops of batter until hard. Place them in an airtight bag and refrigerate for up to 3 days or place in a second freezer bag or airtight container and freeze for up to 3 months. When ready to bake, thaw frozen scoops in the refrigerator. Place scoops on lined pans, bring to room temperature, and bake as directed.

CURRANT AND NIB RUGELACH

Rugelach at its finest is a wondrously flaky yet unbelievably foolproof little horn of pastry pretending to be a cookie. There are various fillings, of which I have always loved the classic—cinnamon, nuts, and raisins—best. So when it turned out that cacao nibs are also good with raisins (or currants), I had to make room for a new favorite.

INGREDIENTS

For the Dough

2½ CUPS (11.25 OUNCES) UNBLEACHED ALL-PURPOSE FLOUR

2 TABLESPOONS SUGAR

¼ TEASPOON SALT

½ POUND (2 STICKS) UNSALTED BUTTER, COLD

8 OUNCES CREAM CHEESE, CHILLED

For the Filling

2 TABLESPOONS GRANULATED SUGAR

½ CUP (3.5 OUNCES) PACKED LIGHT BROWN OR GOLDEN BROWN SUGAR

1 TEASPOON GROUND CINNAMON

½ CUP (2 OUNCES) CACAO NIBS, FINELY CHOPPED

½ CUP (2.5 OUNCES) DRIED CURRANTS

EQUIPMENT

HANDHELD MIXER, STAND MIXER WITH PADDLE ATTACHMENT, OR FOOD PROCESSOR

COOKIE SHEETS, LINED WITH PARCHMENT PAPER OR FOIL

To make the dough with a handheld or stand mixer: Combine the flour, sugar, and salt in a large bowl or in the bowl of a stand mixer fitted with the paddle attachment. Mix briefly to distribute the ingredients. Cut each stick of butter into 8 pieces and add them to the bowl. Mix on low speed (or on medium speed with a handheld mixer) until most of the mixture resembles very coarse bread crumbs, with a few larger pieces of butter the size of hazelnuts. Cut the cream cheese into 1-inch cubes and add them to the bowl. Mix on medium-low speed (medium-high with a handheld mixer) for 30 to 60 seconds, just until the mixture is damp and shaggy looking and holds together when pressed with your fingers.

To make the dough in a food processor: Combine the flour, sugar, and salt in a food processor and pulse a few times to mix. Cut the butter into ¾-inch cubes and add to the flour mixture. Pulse until the butter pieces range in size from coarse bread crumbs to hazelnuts. Cut the cream cheese into 1-inch cubes and add to the mixture. Pulse just until the dough looks damp and shaggy and holds together when pressed with your fingers.

Scrape the dough onto a work surface and knead it two or three times to incorporate any loose pieces. There should be large streaks of cream cheese. Divide the dough into 4 pieces. Press each piece into a flat patty about 4 inches in diameter,

wrap in plastic wrap, and refrigerate until firm, about 4 hours.

Preheat the oven to 350°F. Position racks in the upper and lower thirds of the oven.

To make the filling: Mix the sugars, cinnamon, nuts, and currants together in a medium bowl.

Remove 1 piece of dough from the refrigerator; if necessary, let it stand until pliable enough to roll but not too soft. Roll it out between two sheets of wax paper, plastic wrap, or a cut-up heavy resealable plastic bag into a 12-inch circle a scant ⅛ inch thick. Peel off the top sheet of paper or plastic and place it on the counter or a cutting board. Flip the dough onto the paper or plastic and peel off the second sheet. Sprinkle a quarter of the filling over the dough. Gently roll over the filling with a rolling pin to press it into the dough. Cut the dough into 12 equal wedges like you would a pie. Starting at the wide end of 1 wedge, roll it up and place it, with the dough point underneath to prevent it from unrolling, on one of the cookie sheets. Repeat with the remaining wedges, placing them 1½ inches apart.

Repeat with the remaining dough and filling. (If at any time the dough becomes too soft to roll, return it to the refrigerator to firm up.)

Bake for about 25 minutes or until light golden brown at the edges. Rotate the sheets from top to bottom and from front to back halfway through the baking time to ensure even baking. Set the cookie sheets or just the liners on racks to cool completely. The rugelach are best on the day they are baked, but they can be stored in an airtight container for about 5 days.

LINZER COOKIES

Hearts or stars or scalloped squares—use your imagination with shapes and try different kinds of preserves. Personal favorites are blackberry, raspberry, and apricot. My version of these classic sandwich cookies borrows flavors from the traditional linzer torte: almonds and/or hazelnuts with cinnamon, cloves, and a touch of citrus.

INGREDIENTS

2¼ CUPS (10.125 OUNCES) UNBLEACHED ALL-PURPOSE FLOUR

1 CUP (5 OUNCES) ALMONDS AND/OR HAZELNUTS

½ CUP (3.5 OUNCES) GRANULATED SUGAR

¼ TEASPOON SALT

2½ TEASPOONS GROUND CINNAMON

¼ TEASPOON GROUND CLOVES

½ POUND (2 STICKS) UNSALTED BUTTER

¼ TEASPOON ALMOND EXTRACT

1 TEASPOON GRATED LEMON ZEST OR ¼ TEASPOON LEMON EXTRACT

1 TEASPOON GRATED ORANGE ZEST OR ¼ TEASPOON ORANGE EXTRACT

STRAINED OR PUREED GOOD-QUALITY PRESERVES OR FRUIT SPREAD

POWDERED SUGAR FOR DUSTING

EQUIPMENT

COOKIE SHEETS, LINED WITH PARCHMENT PAPER OR UNGREASED

FOOD PROCESSOR

LARGE AND SMALL COOKIE CUTTERS OF THE SAME OR TWO DIFFERENT SHAPES, SUCH AS A 3-INCH SQUARE AND A 1¼-INCH SQUARE

Combine the flour, nuts, granulated sugar, salt, cinnamon, and cloves in a food processor. Pulse until the nuts are finely ground. Add the butter (cut into several pieces if firm). Pulse until the mixture looks damp and crumbly. Add the almond extract and the lemon and orange zests or extracts and pulse until the mixture begins to clump up around the blade. Remove the dough, press it

into a ball, and knead it a few times to be sure all of the dry ingredients are blended into the dough.

Form the dough into 2 flat patties. Wrap and refrigerate the dough for at least 2 hours and preferably overnight or up to 3 days. The dough may be frozen for up to 3 months.

Preheat the oven to 325°F. Position racks in the upper and lower thirds of the oven.

To roll and cut cookies: Remove 1 patty from the refrigerator and let it sit at room temperature until supple enough to roll but still quite firm. It will continue to soften as you work. Roll the dough to a thickness of ⅛ inch between two sheets of wax paper or between heavy plastic sheets cut from a resealable plastic bag. Turn the dough over once or twice while you are rolling it out to check for deep wrinkles; if necessary, peel off and smooth the paper or plastic over the dough before continuing to roll it. When the dough is thin enough, peel off the top sheet of paper or plastic and keep it in front of you. Invert the dough onto that sheet and peel off the second sheet. Cut as many large shapes as possible. Dip the edges of the cookie cutters in flour as necessary to prevent sticking. Cut a smaller shape from the center of half of the large shapes. Use the point of a paring knife to lift and remove scraps as you transfer the cookies to the lined or ungreased pans. Place large cookies at least 1½ inches apart on the cookie sheets. If the dough gets too soft at any time—while you're rolling, cutting, removing scraps between cookies, or transferring cookies—slide a cookie sheet underneath the paper or plastic and refrigerate the dough for a few minutes, until firm. Repeat with the second patty of dough. Gently press all of the dough scraps together (don't overwork them with too much kneading) and reroll.

Bake for 13 to 15 minutes or until the cookies are just beginning to color at the edges. Rotate the pans from top to bottom and from front to back halfway through the baking time to ensure even baking. (The small shapes may be baked for 8 to 10 minutes on a separate cookie sheet to make miniature cookies, or the dough may be combined with other dough scraps to be rerolled and cut.)

continued

Let the cookies firm up on the pan for 1 to 2 minutes. For lined pans, set the pans or just the liners on racks to cool; for unlined pans, use a metal spatula to transfer the cookies to racks. Cool the cookies completely before stacking or storing. The cookies are delicious fresh but even better the next day. They may be kept in an airtight container for a month or more.

To assemble, shortly before serving, spread each solid cookie with a thin layer of preserves. Sift powdered sugar over the cookies with cutouts. Place a sugared cutout cookie on top of each preserve-covered cookie. Leftover cookies can be stored in an airtight container, but the moisture from the preserves will soften them.

UPGRADE

·····················

Nibby Buckwheat Linzer Hearts: Make the batter for Basic Butter Cookies (page 25), using only 1¼ cups (5.625 ounces) all-purpose flour and mixing it with ¾ cup (3 ounces) buckwheat flour. Mix ⅓ cup (1.33 ounces) roasted cacao nibs and 1 cup (4 ounces) finely chopped walnuts into the batter right before the flour. Cut out the cookies using a 3½-inch heart-shaped cookie cutter and a 1½- or 2-inch heart-shaped cookie cutter. Fill with ½ cup good-quality blackberry or black raspberry preserves.

MY GINGER COOKIES

Also known as Screaming Ginger Cookies. With crunchy edges and a chewy center, beautifully crackled on top, spicy, and loaded with diced crystallized ginger, this is my favorite spice cookie. You can tone down the heat by omitting the fresh ginger and cutting down or the candied ginger and still end up with a great cookie.

INGREDIENTS

2 CUPS (9 OUNCES) UNBLEACHED ALL-PURPOSE FLOUR

2 TEASPOONS BAKING SODA

2 TEASPOONS GROUND GINGER

1½ TEASPOONS GROUND CINNAMON

½ TEASPOON GROUND ALLSPICE

¼ TEASPOON SALT

8 TABLESPOONS (1 STICK) UNSALTED BUTTER, MELTED AND STILL WARM

¼ CUP UNSULFURED (BUT NOT BLACKSTRAP) MILD OR FULL-FLAVORED MOLASSES

½ CUP (3.5 OUNCES) GRANULATED SUGAR

⅓ CUP (2.33 OUNCES) PACKED BROWN SUGAR OR LIGHT MUSCOVADO SUGAR

2 TABLESPOONS FINELY MINCED OR GRATED FRESH GINGER

1 LARGE EGG

¾ CUP (4 OUNCES) GINGER CHIPS OR CRYSTALLIZED GINGER, CUT INTO ¼-INCH DICE *use ½*

ABOUT ½ CUP (3.5 OUNCES) DEMERARA OR TURBINADO SUGAR OR ¼ CUP (1.75 OUNCES) GRANULATED SUGAR FOR ROLLING

EQUIPMENT

COOKIE SHEETS, LINED WITH PARCHMENT PAPER OR UNGREASED

continued

Preheat the oven to 350°F. Position racks in the upper and lower thirds of the oven.

Combine the flour, baking soda, ground ginger, cinnamon, allspice, and salt in a medium bowl and mix thoroughly with a whisk or fork.

Combine the warm butter, molasses, granulated and brown sugars, fresh ginger, and egg in a large bowl and mix thoroughly. Add the flour mixture and ginger chips and stir until incorporated. The dough will be soft.

Form the dough into 1-inch balls (0.5 ounce dough for each). Roll the balls in the Demerara sugar and place them 2 inches apart on the lined or ungreased cookie sheets. Bake for 10 to 12 minutes or until the cookies puff up and crack on the surface and then begin to deflate in the oven. Rotate the sheets from top to bottom and from back to front halfway through the baking time

to ensure even baking. For chewier cookies, remove them from the oven when at least half or more of the cookies have begun to deflate; for crunchier edges with chewy centers, bake for a minute or so longer.

For lined pans, set the pans or just the liners on racks to cool; for unlined pans, use a metal spatula to transfer the cookies to racks. Cool the cookies completely before storing. They may be kept in an airtight container for several days.

UPGRADE

Wheat-Free Ginger Cookies:
Substitute 2 cups (7.25 ounces) oat flour and ½ cup (2.5 ounces) extra-fine white rice flour for the all-purpose flour. Substitute 2 large egg whites for the whole egg. After the flour mixture is completely mixed in, stir briskly for another 40 strokes to aerate the dough slightly.

let dough sit ~ 5 min before rolling

COFFEE WALNUT COOKIES

MAKES ABOUT FORTY-FIVE 2-INCH COOKIES

Walnuts and freshly ground coffee beans make delicately flavored cookies. Coffee lovers might enjoy them with a dish of coffee ice cream and a cup of espresso, but they are also very good with grilled fresh pineapple slices and vanilla ice cream.

INGREDIENTS

2 CUPS (9 OUNCES) UNBLEACHED ALL-PURPOSE FLOUR

1 CUP (3.5 OUNCES) WALNUT HALVES OR PIECES

¾ CUP (5.25 OUNCES) SUGAR

¼ TEASPOON SALT

2 TEASPOONS FRESHLY AND FINELY GROUND MEDIUM-ROAST (NOT ESPRESSO-ROAST) COFFEE BEANS, PLUS ABOUT 45 WHOLE BEANS

12 TABLESPOONS (1½ STICKS) UNSALTED BUTTER

1 TABLESPOON PLUS 1 TEASPOON BRANDY

1½ TEASPOONS PURE VANILLA EXTRACT

EQUIPMENT

COOKIE SHEETS, UNGREASED OR LINED WITH FOIL, DULL SIDE UP

FOOD PROCESSOR

2-INCH COOKIE CUTTER, ROUND OR OTHER SHAPE (OPTIONAL)

Combine the flour, walnuts, sugar, and salt in a food processor and pulse until the walnuts are finely ground. Add the ground coffee and pulse to mix.

Add the butter (cut into several pieces if firm) and pulse until the mixture looks damp and crumbly. Drizzle in the brandy and vanilla and pulse until the dough begins to clump up around the blade. Remove the dough, press it into a ball, and knead it by hand a few times to complete the mixing.

For slice-and-bake cookies, form the dough into a 12-by-2-inch log. (For more petite cookies, or for oval cookies, make a longer, thinner log.) For roll-and-cut cookies, divide the dough in half and form 2 flat patties. Wrap the dough and refrigerate for at least 2 hours and preferably overnight or up to 3 days.

The dough can also be frozen for up to 3 months.

Preheat the oven to 350°F. Position racks in the upper and lower thirds of the oven.

To slice and bake cookies: Use a sharp knife to cut the cold dough log into ¼-inch-thick slices. For oval cookies, slice on the diagonal. (If the dough crumbles when you cut into it, let it soften for several minutes.) Place the cookies at least 1 inch apart on the ungreased or lined pans. Press a coffee bean into the center of each cookie.

To roll and cut cookies: Remove 1 dough patty from the refrigerator and let it stand at room temperature until supple enough to roll but still quite firm; it will continue to soften as you work. Roll the dough to a thickness of ¼ inch between two sheets of wax paper or between heavy plastic sheets cut from a resealable plastic bag. Flip the dough over once or twice while you are rolling it out to check for deep wrinkles; if necessary, peel off and smooth the paper or plastic over the dough before continuing to roll it out. When the dough is thin enough, peel off the top sheet of paper or plastic and place it next to the dough. Invert the dough onto the sheet and peel off the second sheet. Using a cookie cutter, cut out cookies, as close together as possible to minimize scraps, dipping the edges of the cutter in flour as necessary to prevent sticking. Use the point of a paring knife to lift and remove the scraps as you transfer cookies to the lined or ungreased pans, placing them at least 1 inch apart. Press a coffee bean into the center of each. If the dough gets too soft at any time—while you're rolling, cutting, removing scraps between cookies, or transferring the cookies—slide a cookie sheet underneath the paper or plastic and refrigerate the dough for a few minutes, until firm. Repeat with the second patty of dough. Then gently press all of the dough scraps together (without working or kneading them more than necessary), reroll, and cut out more cookies.

Bake the cookies for 12 to 14 minutes, until light golden brown at the edges. Rotate the sheets from top to bottom and from front to back halfway through the baking to ensure even baking.

For lined pans, set the pans or just the liners on racks to cool. For unlined pans, let the cookies firm up on the pans for about 1 minute, then transfer them to a rack with a metal spatula. Cool the cookies completely before stacking or storing. These cookies are delicious fresh but are even better the next day. They may be kept in an airtight container for at least 1 month.

SALTED PEANUT TOFFEE COOKIES

MAKES ABOUT FIFTY-SIX 1½-INCH COOKIES

Encrusted with toffee-coated peanuts and accented with flaky sea salt, these updated peanut butter cookies have a tender melt-in-your-mouth shortbread texture. They are festive enough for a holiday party but easy enough for every day.

INGREDIENTS

1⅓ CUPS (6 OUNCES) UNBLEACHED ALL-PURPOSE FLOUR

½ TEASPOON BAKING SODA

1 TEASPOON FLAKY SEA SALT OR ¾ TEASPOON FINE SEA SALT

8 TABLESPOONS (1 STICK) UNSALTED BUTTER, MELTED

½ CUP (3.5 OUNCES) PACKED LIGHT OR DARK BROWN SUGAR

½ CUP (3.5 OUNCES) GRANULATED SUGAR

1 LARGE EGG

1 TEASPOON PURE VANILLA EXTRACT

1 CUP (9 OUNCES) NATURAL (BUT NOT UNSALTED) CHUNKY PEANUT BUTTER (SEE NOTE)—STIR WELL TO BLEND IN THE OIL BEFORE MEASURING

5 OUNCES STORE-BOUGHT COCONUT TOFFEE PEANUTS OR TOFFEE PEANUTS, COARSELY CHOPPED

EQUIPMENT

COOKIE SHEETS, LINED WITH PARCHMENT PAPER OR GREASED

Combine the flour, baking soda, and salt in a medium bowl and mix together thoroughly with a whisk or fork.

In a large bowl, mix the melted butter with the sugars. Whisk in the egg, vanilla, and peanut butter, add the flour mixture, and mix with a rubber spatula or wooden spoon just until evenly incorporated.

Cover the dough and refrigerate for at least an hour or two and up to 2 days.

continued

Preheat the oven to 325°F. Position racks in the upper and lower thirds of the oven.

Pour the chopped nuts into a shallow bowl. Scoop about 2 level teaspoons of dough for each cookie, shape into a 1-inch ball or a fat little log, and coat the top and sides heavily with the chopped nuts, pressing in any pieces that fall off so that there are no bald spots. Place 2 inches apart on the lined or greased pans.

Bake the cookies for 15 to 18 minutes, until they are lightly colored on top (and underneath). Rotate the sheets from top to bottom and from front to back halfway through the baking time to ensure even baking. The cookies will seem very soft to the touch (and the one you turn over to assess color may even fall apart), but they will firm up as they cool. For lined pans, set the pans or just the liners on racks to cool; for unlined pans, use a metal spatula to transfer the cookies to racks. Cool the cookies completely before storing. They may be kept in an airtight container for at least 2 weeks.

NOTE

By "natural peanut butter," I mean the type that contains only roasted peanuts and (preferably) salt, without sugar, other sweeteners, or emulsifiers. The peanut oil will separate in the jar and must be stirred in well before measuring, but the flavor and consistency are better for my recipes than regular or "no stir" peanut butters.

UPGRADE
....

Salted Peanut Toffee Thumbprints with White Chocolate: Have ready 4 ounces white chocolate cut into little pieces or ⅔ cup (4 ounces) white chocolate chips. Bake the cookies in the shape of balls as described. As soon as the pans come out of the oven, press the back of a chopstick or dowel into the center of each hot cookie and move it around gently to widen the hole. Tuck pieces of chocolate (or chips) into each depression while the cookies are still hot.

BROWNIE BOW TIES

MAKES 48 COOKIES

What more can be said about a flaky pastry filled with an intensely bittersweet bite of chocolate brownie? Just that the flakiest cream cheese dough requires restraint in mixing; yes, you do want to see large streaks of unmixed cream cheese in the dough. Making the dough in a stand mixer yields the best results, but if you use a food processor, follow the method on page 41.

INGREDIENTS

1 RECIPE CURRANT AND NIB RUGELACH CREAM CHEESE DOUGH (PAGE 40)

6 TABLESPOONS UNSALTED BUTTER

4 OUNCES UNSWEETENED CHOCOLATE, COARSELY CHOPPED

1 CUP (7 OUNCES) SUGAR

1 TEASPOON PURE VANILLA EXTRACT

¼ TEASPOON SALT

2 LARGE EGGS, COLD

2 TABLESPOONS UNBLEACHED ALL-PURPOSE FLOUR

A LITTLE MILK FOR BRUSHING ON THE COOKIES

CINNAMON STICK OR NUTMEG FOR GRATING (OPTIONAL)

EQUIPMENT

COOKIE SHEETS, LINED WITH PARCHMENT PAPER OR FOIL

STAND MIXER WITH PADDLE ATTACHMENT OR FOOD PROCESSOR

Make the dough as directed in the recipe on page 40 and chill it.

Melt the butter and chocolate in a heatproof bowl set directly in a wide skillet of barely simmering water. Stir frequently until the mixture is melted and smooth. Remove the bowl from the water. Set aside 2 tablespoons of the sugar. Stir the remaining sugar, the vanilla, and the salt into the chocolate mixture. Whisk in the eggs. Add the flour and

whisk until the mixture is smooth and glossy and cohesive, about 1 minute. Cover and refrigerate until the filling is firm and fudgy, at least 1 hour.

Preheat the oven to 350°F. Position racks in the upper and lower thirds of the oven.

Remove 1 piece of dough from the refrigerator. If the dough is rock-hard, let it sit until it is pliable enough to roll but not too soft. On a floured surface with a floured rolling pin, roll the dough into a 9-by-11-inch rectangle a scant ⅛ inch thick. With a pastry wheel (for nice zigzag edges) or a knife, trim the dough to even the edges. Cut the dough crosswise into quarters and then lengthwise into thirds to make 12 squares. Place a rounded teaspoon (equal to 2 level teaspoons) of chocolate filling in the center of each square. Have a small dish of water at hand. Pick up two opposite corners of a square, moisten the edge of one with a wet fingertip, overlap the corners by about ⅓ inch, and gently press them together over the filling to seal the dough and slightly flatten the filling. Transfer to the lined cookie sheets. Repeat with the remaining squares of dough, arranging the cookies 1½ inches apart. If the dough becomes too soft to handle at any point, refrigerate it briefly to firm it. Roll and fill the remaining pieces of dough. Brush the cookies with just enough milk to moisten them and sprinkle liberally with the reserved 2 tablespoons sugar.

Bake for 18 to 20 minutes, until golden brown. Rotate the pans from top to bottom and from front to back halfway through the baking time to ensure even baking. Set the pans or just the liners on racks to cool. Let the cookies cool completely before stacking or storing. Grate a little cinnamon stick or nutmeg over each cookie before serving, if desired. The cookies may be kept in an airtight container for up to 3 days.

PEANUT BUTTER CLOUDS

Peanut butter folded into meringue makes wonderfully light, crunchy cookies that melt on the tongue with peanut flavor. Make a sundae by piling them into glasses or bowls with vanilla ice cream, sliced strawberries, and unsweetened whipped cream and consider passing a bowl of warm chocolate or caramel sauce . . . and perhaps a pinch of flaky sea salt, such as Maldon or fleur de sel, or other imported or domestic salts available from specialty shops or better supermarkets. Sesame Kisses (see Upgrade) will charm any halvah lover (I'm one). They are marvelous with strawberries and ice cream too, and with a drizzle of honey.

INGREDIENTS

3 EGG WHITES, AT ROOM TEMPERATURE

⅛ TEASPOON CREAM OF TARTAR

⅔ CUP (4.625 OUNCES) SUGAR

⅓ CUP (3 OUNCES) CHUNKY OR SMOOTH NATURAL (BUT NOT SALTED) PEANUT BUTTER (SEE NOTE ON PAGE 55), WELL STIRRED BEFORE MEASURING, AT ROOM TEMPERATURE

3 TABLESPOONS FINELY CHOPPED SALTED PEANUTS

EQUIPMENT

STAND MIXER OR HANDHELD MIXER

COOKIE SHEETS, LINED WITH PARCHMENT PAPER

PASTRY BAG FITTED WITH A ½-INCH OR LARGER PLAIN OR STAR TIP (OPTIONAL)

Preheat the oven to 200°F. Position racks in the upper and lower thirds of the oven.

Combine the egg whites and cream of tartar in a clean dry bowl. Beat at medium-high speed with a heavy-duty stand mixer (or at high speed with a handheld mixer) until the egg whites are creamy white (instead of translucent) and hold a soft shape when the beaters are lifted.

continued

Continue to beat on medium-high speed, adding the sugar a little at a time, taking 1½ to 2 minutes in all, until the whites are very stiff. Scatter small spoonfuls of peanut butter over the meringue. With a large rubber spatula, fold until the peanut butter is imperfectly blended into the meringue; you should see some streaks of white meringue and unmixed peanut butter.

Drop rounded tablespoons of meringue—or use the pastry bag to pipe any size and shape you like—1½ inches apart onto the lined cookie sheets. Sprinkle each meringue with a pinch of the chopped peanuts. Bake for 1½ hours. Rotate the pans from top to bottom and from front to back halfway through the baking time to ensure even baking. Remove a test meringue and let it cool completely before taking a bite. (Meringues are never crisp when hot.) If the meringue is completely dry and crisp, turn off the heat and let the remaining meringues cool completely in the oven. If the test meringue is soft or chewy or sticks to your teeth, bake for another 15 to 20 minutes before testing another meringue.

To prevent the cookies from becoming moist and sticky, put them in an airtight container as soon as they are cool. The meringues may be stored in an airtight container for at least 2 weeks.

UPGRADE

....

Sesame Kisses: Add ½ teaspoon pure vanilla extract or ¾ teaspoon rose water or orange blossom water to the egg whites with the cream of tartar. Substitute ⅓ cup (3 ounces) well-stirred tahini (preferably roasted, not raw), at room temperature, mixed with ⅛ teaspoon salt for the peanut butter. Substitute 2 teaspoons sesame seeds for the chopped peanuts.

PEBBLY BEACH FRUIT SQUARES

MAKES THIRTY-TWO 2½-INCH SQUARE COOKIES

These crunchy-crisp and chewy cookies with sparkling bumpy tops started out to be simple raisin cookies. But you can also make the cookies with prunes, apricots, cherries, dates, cranberries, or candied ginger. Try a ginger/cranberry holiday combo (and note that the cookies are sturdy enough to ship). If dried fruit is especially hard or chewy, it will only get harder after baking. To avoid this, soak pieces in a small bowl with just enough cold water (or fruit juices or wine) to cover for 20 minutes (longer will dilute and oversoften the fruit). Drain and pat pieces very dry before using.

INGREDIENTS

1¾ CUPS PLUS 2 TABLESPOONS (8.5 OUNCES) UNBLEACHED ALL-PURPOSE FLOUR

½ TEASPOON BAKING POWDER

¼ TEASPOON SALT

8 TABLESPOONS (1 STICK) UNSALTED BUTTER

¾ CUP (5.25 OUNCES) GRANULATED SUGAR

1 LARGE EGG

1 TEASPOON PURE VANILLA EXTRACT

1 TEASPOON FINELY GRATED LEMON ZEST OR GROUND CINNAMON OR ANISE

1 GENEROUS CUP MOIST DRIED FRUIT (ONE KIND OR A COMBINATION): DARK OR GOLDEN RAISINS; DRIED SOUR CHERRIES; DRIED CRANBERRIES; COARSELY CHOPPED DATES, DRIED APRICOTS, OR PRUNES; FINELY CHOPPED CANDIED GINGER

2 TO 3 TABLESPOONS TURBINADO OR OTHER COARSE SUGAR

EQUIPMENT

COOKIE SHEETS, LINED WITH PARCHMENT PAPER OR GREASED

continued

Combine the flour, baking powder, and salt in a bowl and mix together thoroughly with a whisk or fork.

With a large spoon in a medium mixing bowl or with a mixer, beat the butter with the granulated sugar until smooth and well blended but not fluffy. Add the egg, vanilla, and lemon zest and beat until smooth. Add the flour mixture and mix until completely incorporated.

Divide the dough in half and form each into a rectangle. Wrap the patties in plastic wrap and refrigerate for at least 2 hours or overnight.

Preheat the oven to 350°F. Position racks in the upper and lower thirds of the oven.

Remove the dough from the refrigerator and let sit for 15 minutes to soften slightly. On a sheet of parchment paper or plastic wrap, roll 1 piece of dough into a rectangle 8½ inches by 16½ inches. With a short side facing you, scatter half of the dried fruit on the bottom half of the dough. Fold the top half

of the dough over the fruit, using the paper as a handle. Peel the paper from the top of the dough. (If it sticks, chill the dough for a few minutes until the paper peels easily.) Dust the top of the dough lightly with flour. Flip the dough onto a lightly floured cutting board and peel off the remaining paper. Sprinkle with half of the coarse sugar and pat lightly to make sure the sugar adheres. Use a heavy knife to trim the edges. Cut into 4 strips and then cut each strip into 4 pieces to make 16 squares. Place the cookies 2 inches apart on the lined or greased pans. Repeat with the remaining dough, fruit, and sugar.

Bake for 12 to 15 minutes or until the edges are lightly browned. Rotate the pans from top to bottom and from front to back halfway through the baking time to ensure even baking. For lined pans, set the pans or just the liners on racks to cool; for unlined pans, use a metal spatula to transfer the cookies to racks. Cool the cookies completely before stacking or storing. They may be kept in an airtight container for a week.

CARDAMOM CARAMEL PALMIERS

MAKES ABOUT 48 COOKIES

Both flaky and crunchy, these are a much quicker and easier version of a very classic and elegant pastry, normally made without the cardamom, which a purist may choose to omit. Using a stand mixer yields flakier pastry, but I've also provided a food processor method.

INGREDIENTS

For the Dough

2½ CUPS (11.25 OUNCES) UNBLEACHED ALL-PURPOSE FLOUR

2 TABLESPOONS SUGAR

¼ TEASPOON SALT

½ POUND (2 STICKS) UNSALTED BUTTER, COLD

8 OUNCES CREAM CHEESE, COLD

For the Filling

1 CUP (7 OUNCES) SUGAR

1 TEASPOON GROUND CARDAMOM

2 PINCHES OF SALT

EQUIPMENT

COOKIE SHEETS, UNGREASED OR LINED WITH FOIL, DULL SIDE UP

STAND MIXER WITH PADDLE ATTACHMENT OR FOOD PROCESSOR

To make the dough in a stand mixer: Combine the flour, sugar, and salt in the mixer bowl. Using the paddle attachment, mix briefly to distribute the ingredients. Cut each stick of butter into 8 pieces and add them to the bowl. Mix on low speed until most of the mixture resembles very coarse bread crumbs with a few larger pieces of butter the size of hazelnuts. Cut the cream cheese into 1-inch cubes and add them to the bowl. Mix on medium-low speed until the mixture is damp and shaggy looking and holds together when pressed with your fingers, 30 to 60 seconds.

continued

To make the dough in a food processor: Combine the flour, sugar, and salt in a food processor and pulse a few times to mix. Cut the butter into ¾-inch cubes and add to the flour mixture. Pulse until the butter pieces range in size from coarse bread crumbs to hazelnuts. Cut the cream cheese into 1-inch cubes and add to the mixture. Pulse until the dough looks damp and shaggy and holds together when pressed with your fingers.

Dump the dough onto the work surface, scraping the bowl. Knead two or three times to incorporate any loose pieces. There should be large streaks of cream cheese.

Divide the dough into 2 equal pieces and shape each into a 4-by-5-inch rectangular patty about 1 inch thick. Wrap and chill the dough until firm, at least 2 hours and up to 3 days.

Remove the dough from the refrigerator. If necessary, let the dough sit at room temperature until pliable enough to roll but not too soft.

To make the filling: Mix the sugar with the cardamom. Transfer 2 tablespoons of the mixture to a cup and mix thoroughly with the salt. Set aside (for the baking step).

Divide the remaining cardamom sugar equally between two bowls; you will use one bowl for each piece of dough you roll out.

Sprinkle the work surface liberally with some of the cardamom sugar from one of the bowls Set 1 piece of dough on the sugared surface and sprinkle it with more cardamom sugar. Turn the dough frequently and resugar it and the work surface liberally as you roll the dough into a 24-by-8-inch rectangle that's less than ⅛ inch thick. Use the cardamom sugar generously to prevent sticking and to ensure that the cookies will caramelize properly in the oven. Trim the edges of the rectangle evenly.

Mark the center of the dough with a small indentation. Starting at one short edge, fold about 2½ inches of dough almost one-third of the distance to the center mark. Without stretching or pulling, loosely fold the dough over two more times, leaving a scant ¼-inch space at the center mark. Likewise, fold the other end of the dough toward the center three times, leaving a tiny space at the center. The dough should now resemble a tall, narrow open book. Fold one side of the dough over the other side, as if closing the book. You should have an 8-layer strip of dough about 2½ inches wide and 8 inches long.

Sprinkle the remaining cardamom sugar under and on top of the dough. Roll gently from one end of the dough to the other to compress the layers and lengthen the strip to about 9 inches. Wrap the dough loosely in wax paper (plastic wrap might cause moisture to dissolve the sugar on the outside of the dough). Refrigerate the dough for at least 30 minutes and up to 4 hours. Repeat with the second piece of dough and the second bowl of cardamom sugar.

Preheat the oven to 375°F. Position racks in the upper and lower thirds of the oven.

Remove 1 piece of dough from the refrigerator, unwrap it, and use a sharp knife to trim the ends evenly. Cut ⅛-inch slices (I mark the dough at 1-inch intervals and cut 3 slices from each inch) and arrange them 1½ inches apart on the ungreased or lined cookie sheets. Bake for 8 to 10 minutes, until the undersides are deep golden brown. Rotate the pans from top to bottom and from front to back halfway through the baking time to ensure even baking.

Remove the pans from the oven. Turn the cookies over. Sprinkle each with a pinch or two of the salted cardamom sugar, reserving half of it for the second round. Return the sheets to the oven and bake for 3 to 5 more minutes, until the cookies are deep golden brown. Rotate the pans and watch the cookies carefully to prevent burning. If the cookies brown at different rates, remove the dark ones and let the lighter ones continue to bake. For lined pans, set the pans or just the liners on racks to cool; for unlined pans, use a metal spatula to transfer the cookies to racks. Making sure the cookie sheets are completely cool, repeat with the second piece of dough. Cool the cookies completely before storing. They may be kept in an airtight container for up to 4 days.

NEW CLASSIC COCONUT MACAROONS

Always a fan of golden-brown sweet, toasty coconut macaroons with moist, chewy centers, I was excited to reinvent them using wide shaved flakes of unsweetened dried coconut instead of the usual sweetened (alas, always artificially preserved) shreds. They turned out more stunningly beautiful than ever, and the flavor is pure coconut. Default to the classic recipe, using the sweetened shreds, and keep the same sugar measure (trust me). Either way, don't miss the sensational version with a nuance of lime zest and cinnamon.

INGREDIENTS

4 LARGE EGG WHITES

3½ CUPS (5.25 OUNCES) UNSWEETENED DRIED FLAKED (NOT SHREDDED) COCONUT, ALSO CALLED COCONUT CHIPS, OR 3 CUPS (9 OUNCES) SWEETENED DRIED SHREDDED COCONUT (SEE NOTE)

¾ CUP (5.25 OUNCES) SUGAR

2 TEASPOONS PURE VANILLA EXTRACT

SLIGHTLY ROUNDED ¼ TEASPOON SALT

EQUIPMENT

COOKIE SHEETS, LINED WITH PARCHMENT PAPER

Combine all of the ingredients in a large heatproof mixing bowl, preferably stainless steel because the mixture will heat faster than in glass. Set the bowl directly in a wide skillet of barely simmering water and stir the mixture with a silicone spatula, scraping the bottom to prevent burning, until the mixture is very hot to the touch and the egg whites have thickened slightly and turned from translucent to opaque, 5 to 7 minutes. Set the batter aside for 30 minutes to let the coconut absorb more of the goop.

continued

Preheat the oven to 350°F. Position racks in the upper and lower thirds of the oven.

Using 2 tablespoons of batter, make attractive heaps 2 inches apart on the lined cookie sheets. Bake for about 5 minutes, just until the coconut tips begin to color, rotating the pans from top to bottom and from front to back halfway through the baking time to ensure even baking. Lower the temperature to 325°F and bake for 10 to 15 minutes, until the cookies are a beautiful cream and gold with deeper brown edges, again rotating the pans from top to bottom and from front to back halfway through the baking time. If the coconut tips are browning too fast, you can lower the heat to 300°F. Set the pans or just the liners on racks to cool. Let cool completely before gently peeling the parchment away from each cookie. The cookies are best on the day they are baked—the exterior is crisp and chewy and the interior soft and moist. Although the crispy edges will soften, the cookies remain delicious stored in an airtight container for 4 to 5 days.

NOTE

Unsweetened dried shredded coconut and wide strips of dried shaved unsweetened coconut (aka coconut chips) both have super true coconut flavor in cookies, and neither has the preservatives and sugar. Both are found in better supermarkets, in specialty markets that sell nuts and dried fruit in bulk, in natural food stores, and online (see Resources). The flavor and quality make it worth finding. Sweetened dried shredded coconut is a supermarket staple found in the baking aisle.

UPGRADES
....

Coconut Macaroons with Lime Zest and Cinnamon: Stir 1½ to 2 teaspoons freshly grated lime zest into the batter before scooping it. Using a fine grater or Microplane zester, grate a little cinnamon stick over the cookies just before serving.

Coconut Banana Macaroons: Crush unsweetened freeze-dried banana slices to make a scant 2 tablespoons of banana powder. Add the powder to the ingredients before mixing and heating.

VANILLA CREAM CHEESE SANDWICHES

Cookies *à la minute*? Sweet, extra-crunchy vanilla cookies are filled, just before serving, with cream cheese, mascarpone, or creamy Greek-style yogurt, then drizzled with a little honey. Nibble them out of hand or plate them (with a scattering of berries?) like tartlets for an appealing little dessert or teatime indulgence. I can't help admitting that plain yogurt is more exciting with the sweet cookie and sticky honey than the more decadent mascarpone. You have to love it when the least expensive and least fattening choice actually tastes the best!

INGREDIENTS

3 CUPS (13.5 OUNCES) UNBLEACHED ALL-PURPOSE FLOUR

2 TEASPOONS CREAM OF TARTAR

1 TEASPOON BAKING SODA

½ TEASPOON SALT

½ POUND (2 STICKS) UNSALTED BUTTER, SOFTENED

1½ CUPS (10.5 OUNCES) SUGAR

2 TABLESPOONS MILK

1 TABLESPOON PURE VANILLA EXTRACT

VANILLA SUGAR (RECIPE FOLLOWS) FOR SPRINKLING

1 POUND CREAM CHEESE, MASCARPONE, OR GREEK-STYLE YOGURT (OR REGULAR YOGURT, DRAINED FOR SEVERAL HOURS TO REMOVE EXTRA LIQUID)

HONEY FOR DRIZZLING (OPTIONAL)

EQUIPMENT

COOKIE SHEETS, LINED WITH PARCHMENT PAPER OR GREASED

3-INCH ROUND COOKIE CUTTER

1½-INCH ROUND COOKIE CUTTER

STAND MIXER WITH PADDLE ATTACHMENT OR HANDHELD MIXER

continued

Combine the flour, cream of tartar, baking soda, and salt in a bowl and mix together thoroughly with a whisk or fork.

In the bowl of a stand mixer fitted with the paddle attachment, or in a large mixing bowl with a handheld mixer, beat the butter with the sugar until smooth and creamy. Beat in the milk and vanilla. Add the flour mixture and stir or beat on low speed just until incorporated. The dough will be very soft.

Divide the dough into 2 pieces. Gently roll the first piece ⅛ inch thick between two sheets of wax paper. Slide the whole business onto a cookie sheet. Repeat with the second piece of dough, sliding it onto the cookie sheet on top of the first piece. Refrigerate the dough for at least 2 hours or overnight.

Preheat the oven to 350°F. Position racks in the upper and lower thirds of the oven.

Remove 1 sheet of dough from the fridge. Peel off the top piece of wax paper and sprinkle the dough with a little flour. Put the wax paper loosely back over the dough and flip the dough and both sheets of wax paper over. Peel off the top sheet of wax paper. Cut out 3-inch rounds of dough. Cut 1½-inch circles from half of the rounds and remove them with a fork or with the point of a paring knife. (Combine and save scraps and small rounds.) Transfer the cookies to the lined or greased cookie sheets about 1½ inches apart. Sprinkle the cookies with holes in them with pinches of vanilla sugar. Bake for 10 to 12 minutes, until golden, rotating the sheets from top to bottom and from front to back halfway through the baking time to ensure even baking.

For lined pans, set the pans or just the liners on racks to cool; for unlined pans, use a metal spatula to transfer the cookies to racks. Cool the cookies completely before stacking, filling, or storing. Repeat with the remaining rolled-out dough until all the cookies are baked. Combine all the scraps, roll, chill, cut, and bake as described.

The cookies may be stored in an airtight container for several days.

THE ARTISANAL KITCHEN: *Holiday Cookies*

Just before serving, mix the cream cheese, if using, with a rubber spatula until creamy and easy to spread. Spread the solid cookies liberally with the cheese or yogurt. Top with the remaining cookies. Drizzle with honey, if desired.

Vanilla Sugar

MAKES 2 CUPS

Keep this on hand for baking, to sprinkle on fruit or cereal, and to mix into anything that will taste good sweetened with vanilla.

INGREDIENTS

1 WHOLE VANILLA BEAN OR PIECES OF SCRAPED BEAN LEFT OVER FROM OTHER COOKING, OR 1 TEASPOON OR MORE GROUND OR POWDERED VANILLA BEAN

2 CUPS (14 OUNCES) SUGAR

If using a whole vanilla bean, slice down the middle and scrape the seeds into the sugar. Stir well and put the sugar in a jar with the scraped bean pieces. Or stir the ground or powdered vanilla into the sugar. In a week or so, the sugar will be fragrant and flavorful. If you use a little vanilla sugar at a time, and not too frequently, you can replace the amount taken out with more plain sugar, stirring it in well.

STICKY PECAN BITES

MAKES 24 ROLLS

Rich, tender, cakey, with a bit of caramely brown sugar goop. Think bite-sized sticky buns without the time-consuming yeast dough. These little cheaters are made with a quick stirred-together cream biscuit concoction. Too simple for words.

INGREDIENTS

24 PECAN HALVES

1 CUP (4.5 OUNCES) UNBLEACHED ALL-PURPOSE FLOUR

1 TEASPOON BAKING POWDER

¼ TEASPOON SALT, PLUS EXTRA FOR SPRINKLING

¾ CUP HEAVY CREAM

½ CUP (3.5 OUNCES) PACKED BROWN OR MUSCOVADO SUGAR

½ TEASPOON GROUND CINNAMON

2 TABLESPOONS UNSALTED BUTTER, VERY SOFT

EQUIPMENT

1 MINIATURE MUFFIN PAN WITH 24 CUPS OR 2 MINIATURE MUFFIN PANS WITH 12 CUPS EACH

Preheat the oven to 400°F. Position a rack in the lower third of the oven. Lightly grease the muffin cups unless they are nonstick pans.

Place a pecan half in each cup, top side down. Combine the flour, baking powder, and ¼ teaspoon salt in a medium bowl and mix together thoroughly with a whisk or fork. Make a well in the center. Pour the cream into the well. Use a rubber spatula to fold and stir the flour mixture and cream together just until the dry ingredients are entirely moistened and a soft dough is formed; it should not look perfectly smooth. Let the dough rest for 2 to 3 minutes to firm up. Meanwhile, mix the sugar with the cinnamon.

continued

On a lightly floured surface, with a floured rolling pin, roll the dough to a rectangle 12 by 7 inches and ¼ inch thick. Spread the dough with the soft butter and sprinkle with a pinch of salt and the brown sugar. Starting at one short end, roll the dough tightly. Gently stretch the dough to lengthen the roll. Cut the roll crosswise into 24 equal pieces. Place each piece in a muffin cup, cut side up.

Bake for 12 to 15 minutes, until well browned. Rotate the pan(s) from front to back halfway through the baking time to ensure even baking.

Immediately turn the cookies out onto a sheet of parchment on a heatproof surface. Serve on the day you make them.

UPGRADE

Chocolate Roll-Ups: Omit the pecans, cinnamon, and butter. Spread the dough with a mixture of ½ cup sour cream and ¼ cup packed brown sugar. Sprinkle evenly with 1¾ ounces finely chopped semisweet or bittersweet chocolate with 55% to 62% cacao.

MEXICAN WEDDING CAKES

Tender nut-studded round or crescent-shaped cookies rolled in powdered sugar turn up around the globe; only the nuts and the names are different. Use pecans to make Mexican Wedding Cakes (aka *polvorones*), almonds for Viennese crescents or Greek *kourabiedes*, and walnuts for Russian tea cakes. Try toasted and skinned hazelnuts, macadamias, Brazil nuts, hickory nuts, pistachios, or peanuts . . .

There are both ground nuts and crunchy chopped nuts in this recipe. If you prefer all the nuts to be ground—for an even more tender, melt-in-your-mouth cookie—skip the first paragraph of the instructions. After pulverizing the sugar, put all the nuts into the processor with the flour and salt and pulse until the nuts are all finely ground.

INGREDIENTS

1½ CUPS NUTS

¼ CUP (1.75 OUNCES) GRANULATED SUGAR

2 CUPS (9 OUNCES) UNBLEACHED ALL-PURPOSE FLOUR

½ TEASPOON SALT

½ POUND (2 STICKS) UNSALTED BUTTER, SOFTENED AND CUT INTO SMALL CHUNKS

2 TEASPOONS PURE VANILLA EXTRACT

1 LARGE EGG YOLK (OPTIONAL)

½ CUP (1.5 OUNCES) POWDERED SUGAR

EQUIPMENT

COOKIE SHEETS, LINED WITH PARCHMENT PAPER OR UNGREASED

FOOD PROCESSOR

continued

Pulse the nuts in a food processor until half of them look pulverized and the rest look chopped. Transfer the nuts to a bowl and set aside. Wipe the bowl of the food processor with a paper towel to remove excess oil from the nuts.

Put the granulated sugar in the processor and process until it is fine and powdery. Add the flour and salt and pulse just to mix. Add the butter, the vanilla, and the egg yolk, if using. Process until the mixture looks damp and begins to clump together. Add the nuts and pulse just until combined. Transfer the dough to a bowl. Cover and refrigerate the dough for at least 2 hours and preferably overnight.

Preheat the oven to 325°F. Position racks in the upper and lower thirds of the oven.

Shape slightly more than level tablespoons of dough into 1¼-inch balls or crescent shapes. Place the cookies 2 inches apart on the lined or ungreased pans. Bake for 22 to 24 minutes or until lightly colored on top and golden brown on the bottom. Rotate the cookie sheets from top to bottom and from front to back halfway through the baking time to ensure even baking.

Let the cookies cool on the pan for 5 minutes and then sieve powdered sugar over them. For lined pans, set the pans or just the liners on racks to finish cooling; for unlined pans, use a metal spatula to transfer the cookies to a rack. Cool the cookies completely before storing. They may be stored in an airtight container for at least 2 weeks. Sieve additional powdered sugar over the cookies before serving if necessary.

UPGRADE

Nutty Thumbprint Cookies:
Shape the dough into balls. Dip the handle of a wooden spoon (or your finger) in flour and press it into each ball to form a depression. Bake and cool as directed. Fill with chocolate ganache or Nutella; alternatively, shortly before serving, fill with jam, preserves, lemon curd, or dulce de leche. You will need at least ½ cup of filling for 48 cookies.

HOLIDAY SPICE BATONS

Flavorful and elegant. Fun to make. Kids can help scatter sugar and spices and roll up the dough. Each version is a little flavor story. Feel free to divide this large recipe in half to make only 40 pieces. Wrap and refreeze the remaining dough or use it to make a half recipe of one of the Upgrades or half of another recipe that calls for phyllo dough.

INGREDIENTS

2 TEASPOONS GROUND CINNAMON

½ TEASPOON GROUND CLOVES

1 CUP (7 OUNCES) SUGAR

2 TEASPOONS FINELY GRATED ORANGE ZEST

1 POUND PHYLLO DOUGH, AT ROOM TEMPERATURE

½ POUND (2 STICKS) UNSALTED BUTTER, MELTED

EQUIPMENT

COOKIE SHEETS, LINED WITH PARCHMENT PAPER OR FOIL

Preheat the oven to 350°F. Position racks in the upper and lower thirds of the oven.

Combine the cinnamon, cloves, sugar, and orange zest in a small bowl and mix thoroughly. Place 1 sheet of phyllo dough on a smooth surface. Use a spoon to drizzle some melted butter all over the surface of the dough, using only the clear yellow portion of the butter and not the milky white part. Use a brush or your fingers to spread the butter over the entire sheet of dough, gently sliding and patting the butter. Add more butter if necessary. Cut the dough into rectangles about 6 by 8 inches.

Sprinkle each rectangle with about ½ teaspoon of the sugar and spice mixture. Starting from one of the long edges, turn over about ½ inch of dough and roll 2 turns. Fold each side to the center and continue rolling; the finished roll will be 4 inches long and ½ inch thick. Place seam side down on one of the lined pans. Repeat with the remaining dough and sugar and spice mixture, placing the cookies about ½ inch apart. For extra sparkle, you can brush the rolls with butter and sprinkle with any leftover sugar mixture or plain sugar.

Bake for 10 to 15 minutes, until both tops and bottoms are golden brown. Rotate the pans from top to bottom and from front to back halfway through the baking time to ensure even baking. Set the pans or just the liners on racks to cool. Let the cookies cool completely before stacking or storing. They may be kept in an airtight container for up to 5 days.

UPGRADES

Scandinavian Spice Batons: Substitute for the sugar and spice mixture: 1 teaspoon ground cardamom, 1 teaspoon freshly grated nutmeg, 1 cup (7 ounces) sugar, and 2 teaspoons finely grated lemon zest.

Sesame Batons: Substitute for the sugar and spice mixture: 1 cup (7 ounces) sugar and 1 cup (5 ounces) sesame seeds; use 1 teaspoon of filling per cookie.

TWICE-BAKED SHORTBREAD

MAKES FOURTEEN TO SIXTEEN 2-INCH SQUARES, OR 16 WEDGES

There are a couple of secrets to this tender, buttery, crunchy shortbread. For the best flavor and texture, let the dough rest in the pan for at least 2 hours or overnight before baking. A second short bake toasts each piece ever so slightly, adding extra flavor and resulting in a light, crunchier texture through and through. Shortbread keeps for many weeks in a sealed container, and it makes a wonderful gift.

INGREDIENTS

11 TABLESPOONS UNSALTED BUTTER, MELTED AND STILL WARM

¼ CUP PLUS 1 TABLESPOON (2.125 OUNCES) GRANULATED SUGAR

1 TEASPOON PURE VANILLA EXTRACT

¼ TEASPOON SALT

1½ CUPS (6.75 OUNCES) UNBLEACHED ALL-PURPOSE FLOUR

TURBINADO, DEMERARA, OR GRANULATED SUGAR FOR SPRINKLING

EQUIPMENT

8-INCH SQUARE BAKING PAN OR 9½-INCH ROUND FLUTED TART PAN WITH A REMOVABLE BOTTOM

COOKIE SHEET, LINED WITH PARCHMENT PAPER

Line the bottom and sides of the baking pan with foil (see page 19) or grease the tart pan.

In a medium bowl, combine the melted butter with the sugar, vanilla, and salt. Add the flour and mix just until incorporated. Pat and spread the dough evenly in the pan. Let rest for at least 2 hours or overnight (no need to refrigerate).

Preheat the oven to 300°F. Position a rack in the lower third of the oven.

Bake the shortbread for 45 minutes. Remove the pan from the oven, leaving the oven on. Lightly sprinkle the surface of the shortbread with sugar. Let the shortbread cool for 10 minutes.

Remove the shortbread from the pan, taking care to avoid breaking it. Use a thin sharp knife to cut it into oblong "fingers," wedges, or squares. Place the pieces slightly apart on the parchment-lined pan and bake for 15 minutes. Cool the shortbread on a rack. It may be kept in an airtight container for several weeks.

UPGRADE

....

Bourbon Pecan or Peanut Shortbread: Decrease the flour to 1¼ cups. Add ½ cup (1.75 ounces) pecans or roasted peanuts (salted or not). Substitute packed brown sugar for the granulated sugar and add 1 tablespoon bourbon with the vanilla. If using salted peanuts, omit the salt from the recipe.

ROCKY ROAD BARS

These are gooey and chewy—definitely a recipe to make with kids. But try it on friends who think they are too sophisticated to appreciate chocolate with marshmallows and nuts on a graham cracker crust. Use an oiled knife to cut the marshmallows. This is a little more work than buying miniature marshmallows, but the results will be more delicious.

INGREDIENTS

6 TABLESPOONS UNSALTED BUTTER, MELTED

1½ CUPS (5 OUNCES) FINE GRAHAM CRACKER CRUMBS (MADE FROM ABOUT 9 DOUBLE GRAHAM CRACKERS)

¼ CUP (1.75 OUNCES) SUGAR

1 CUP (3.5 OUNCES) WALNUT HALVES OR LARGE PIECES

12 REGULAR MARSHMALLOWS (3.25 OUNCES), QUARTERED

1 CUP (6 OUNCES) MILK CHOCOLATE OR SEMISWEET CHOCOLATE CHIPS

EQUIPMENT

8-INCH SQUARE PAN, THE BOTTOM AND ALL 4 SIDES LINED WITH FOIL (SEE PAGE 19)

Preheat the oven to 350°F. Position racks in the upper and lower thirds of the oven.

Mix the butter with the graham cracker crumbs and sugar until all of the crumbs are moistened. Turn the mixture into the lined pan and spread it evenly, pressing very firmly all over the bottom to form a crust. Scatter half of the nut pieces evenly over the crust.

Bake on the lower oven rack for 10 minutes or until the crust begins to turn golden brown. Remove from the oven and scatter the marshmallows, chocolate chips, and remaining walnuts evenly over the crust. Turn the oven temperature up to 375°F, return the pan to the oven on the upper rack, and bake for 10 to 12 minutes, until the marshmallows are golden brown and merged with one another. Set on a rack to cool completely. Lift the ends of the foil liner and transfer the bars to a cutting board. Use a long sharp knife to cut into sixteen 2-inch bars. The bars may be kept in an airtight container for 4 to 5 days.

UPGRADES
....

You can use chocolate graham crackers, plain chocolate wafers, or purchased gingersnaps instead of the graham crackers. You can add ¼ teaspoon ground cinnamon to the crust mixture. You can swap pecans or any other nuts for the walnuts. You could grate some cinnamon stick or nutmeg on top or sprinkle with tiny pinches of cardamom. . . .

ROBERT'S BROWNIES MY WAY

MAKES SIXTEEN 2-INCH BROWNIES

I resist the term *fudgy*—it is inadequate for these exceptional brownies. They are densely creamy and intensely bittersweet beneath a paper-thin nuance of crust on top.

The late Robert Steinberg (cofounder of Scharffen Berger Chocolate Maker) created the recipe for the company's first chocolate, Scharffen Berger Bittersweet 70% Chocolate. This remains a go-to modern recipe for very chocolaty brownies that are not excessively sweet.

INGREDIENTS

6 TABLESPOONS UNSALTED BUTTER

8 OUNCES BITTERSWEET CHOCOLATE WITH 70% CACAO

1 SCANT CUP (6.5 OUNCES) SUGAR

¼ TEASPOON SALT

½ TEASPOON PURE VANILLA EXTRACT (OPTIONAL)

2 LARGE EGGS, COLD

⅓ CUP PLUS 1 TABLESPOON (1.75 OUNCES) UNBLEACHED ALL-PURPOSE FLOUR

1 CUP (3.5 OUNCES) WALNUT OR PECAN PIECES (OPTIONAL)

EQUIPMENT

8-INCH SQUARE PAN, THE BOTTOM AND ALL 4 SIDES LINED WITH FOIL (SEE PAGE 19)

Preheat the oven to 350°F. Position a rack in the lower third of the oven.

Melt the butter with the chocolate in a medium heatproof bowl set directly in a wide skillet of barely simmering water. Stir frequently until the mixture is melted and smooth and fairly hot to the touch. Remove the bowl from the water. Stir in the sugar, the salt, and the vanilla, if using. Add

1 egg, stirring until it is incorporated. Repeat with the second egg. Stir in the flour and beat with a wooden spoon or spatula until the batter is smooth and glossy and comes away from the sides of the pan; it is critical that the batter pull itself together, so don't stop mixing until it does. Stir in the nuts, if using. Scrape the batter into the pan.

Spread the batter evenly but with lots of raised swirls and ridges—these look great and get slightly crusty in the oven. Bake for 30 to 35 minutes, until a toothpick inserted in the center comes out with a few moist crumbs, not totally gooey.

Cool on a rack. Lift the foil ends to transfer the brownies to a cutting board. Cut into 16 squares. The brownies may be kept in an airtight container for 2 to 3 days.

CARAMEL CHEESECAKE BARS

MAKES THIRTY-SIX 1½-BY-2-INCH BARS

Creamy and gooey! Rich vanilla cheesecake, slightly tangy, laced with sweet salted caramel. The flavor and texture of cheesecake only gets better, so make these a day or two ahead if you can.

INGREDIENTS

1 RECIPE SHORTBREAD CRUST
(RECIPE FOLLOWS)

½ CUP (6 OUNCES) CARAMEL SAUCE,
PURCHASED OR HOMEMADE

⅛ TEASPOON SALT

1½ POUNDS CREAM CHEESE,
AT ROOM TEMPERATURE

¼ CUP (1.75 OUNCES) SUGAR

1½ TEASPOONS PURE
VANILLA EXTRACT

2 LARGE EGGS,
AT ROOM TEMPERATURE

EQUIPMENT

9-BY-13-INCH METAL BAKING PAN OR
8-BY-12-INCH QUARTER SHEET PAN,
THE BOTTOM AND ALL 4 SIDES LINED
WITH FOIL (SEE PAGE 19)

STAND MIXER WITH PADDLE
ATTACHMENT OR HANDHELD MIXER

Prepare the shortbread crust.

Preheat the oven to 325°F.

Stir the caramel sauce together with the salt. Set aside.

In the bowl of a stand mixer fitted with the paddle attachment, or in a medium mixing bowl with a handheld mixer, beat the cream cheese just until smooth, about 30 seconds. Scrape the bowl and beaters. Add the sugar and vanilla and beat just until smooth and creamy, 1 to 2 minutes. Add 1 egg and beat just until incorporated. Scrape the bowl and beaters. Beat in the second egg. Stir 2 tablespoons of the batter into the caramel sauce. Pour the remaining batter over the prepared crust and smooth the top.

Spoon pools of the caramel mixture over the filling, leaving plenty of plain filling showing. If the caramel does not settle into the batter, jiggle the pan gently until the surface is level. Marble the caramel with a toothpick by stirring gently—being careful not to scrape the crust—in small loopy circles until the colors are marbled but not blended. Bake for 20 to 25 minutes, until the filling is puffed at the edges but still jiggles like Jell-O when the pan is nudged.

Set the pan on a cooling rack. When the bars are completely cool, cover and refrigerate the bars until set, at least 4 hours, but preferably 24 hours, before serving. To serve, lift the edges of the foil liner and transfer to a cutting board. Use a long sharp knife to cut into bars 1½ by 2 inches. The bars may be kept in an airtight container, refrigerated, for up to 4 days.

UPGRADE

Peanut Caramel Cheesecake Bars: Use only a scant ½ cup of caramel sauce. Mix ⅓ cup (3 ounces) well-stirred creamy natural peanut butter (see Note on page 55) into the sauce with the salt. Do not add any of the cheesecake batter to the caramel mixture. If the mixture is too thick or stiff to flow (slightly) from a spoon, warm it briefly in a pan of hot water or for a few seconds in the microwave. Use as directed.

Shortbread Crust

Tender, buttery, crunchy, this is a great base for cheesecake bars, pudding bars, and more.

INGREDIENTS

14 TABLESPOONS (1¾ STICKS) UNSALTED BUTTER, MELTED AND STILL WARM

½ CUP (3.5 OUNCES) SUGAR

2 TEASPOONS PURE VANILLA EXTRACT

⅜ TEASPOON SALT

2 CUPS (9 OUNCES) UNBLEACHED ALL-PURPOSE FLOUR

Preheat the oven to 350°F. Position a rack in the lower third of the oven. Line all 4 sides of the pan specified in the individual recipe with foil (see page 19).

In a medium bowl, mix the melted butter with the sugar, vanilla, and salt. Add the flour and mix just until incorporated. Don't worry if the dough seems too soft or oily. Press and smooth the dough evenly over the bottom of the pan. Bake for 20 to 25 minutes, until the crust is a rich golden brown with well-browned darker edges. Let cool on a rack before proceeding as directed in the recipe.

VERY TANGY
LEMON BARS

An esteemed New England cooking magazine once pronounced my lemon bars too sour, though my cooking students and guests continue to declare them the best ever. Perhaps it's a New England versus California thing. I mention this so you will know what you are getting into here: very special (and very tangy) citrus bars with a tender, crunchy crust.

INGREDIENTS

For the Crust

7 TABLESPOONS UNSALTED BUTTER, MELTED

2 TABLESPOONS SUGAR

¾ TEASPOON PURE VANILLA EXTRACT

¼ TEASPOON SALT

1 CUP (4.5 OUNCES) UNBLEACHED ALL-PURPOSE FLOUR

For the Topping

1 CUP PLUS 2 TABLESPOONS (7.875 OUNCES) GRANULATED SUGAR

3 TABLESPOONS UNBLEACHED ALL-PURPOSE FLOUR

3 LARGE EGGS

1½ TEASPOONS FINELY GRATED LEMON ZEST (SEE NOTE), PREFERABLY FROM AN ORGANIC OR UNSPRAYED FRUIT

½ CUP STRAINED FRESH LEMON JUICE (SEE NOTE), PREFERABLY FROM AN ORGANIC OR UNSPRAYED FRUIT

POWDERED SUGAR FOR DUSTING (OPTIONAL)

EQUIPMENT

8-INCH SQUARE METAL BAKING PAN, THE BOTTOM AND ALL 4 SIDES LINED WITH FOIL (SEE PAGE 19)

continued

Preheat the oven to 350°F. Position a rack in the lower third of the oven.

To make the crust: In a medium bowl, combine the melted butter with the sugar, vanilla, and salt. Add the flour and mix just until incorporated. Press the dough evenly over the bottom of the pan.

Bake for 25 to 30 minutes or until the crust is fully baked, well browned at the edges, and golden brown in the center.

To make the topping: While the crust is baking, stir together the sugar and flour in a large bowl until well mixed. Whisk in the eggs. Stir in the lemon zest and juice.

When the crust is ready, turn the oven down to 300°F. Slide the rack with the pan out and pour the filling onto the hot crust. Bake for 20 to 25 minutes longer or until the topping barely jiggles in the center when the pan is tapped.

Set on a rack to cool completely in the pan.

Lift up the foil liner and transfer the bars to a cutting board. If the surface is covered with a thin layer of moist foam (not unusual), you can blot it gently to reveal the zest by laying a square of paper towel on the surface and gently sweeping your fingers over it to absorb excess moisture. Remove the paper and repeat with a fresh piece if necessary. Use a long sharp knife to cut into sixteen 2-inch or 25 daintier bars. Sift powdered sugar over the bars just before serving, if desired. The bars may be stored in an airtight container in the refrigerator for several days or more. After 3 days the crust softens, but the bars still taste quite good for up to a week.

NOTE
Meyer lemons are less tart and more floral than most other lemons. If you want to use them, reduce the sugar in the topping to ½ cup plus 2 tablespoons (4.375 ounces).

MAYA'S NO-NO-NANAIMO BARS

MAKES 16 LARGE (2¼-INCH) BARS OR 25 SMALLER BARS

Named after the city in British Columbia, the traditional Nanaimo bar is a no-bake affair with a crumb crust and layers of sweet vanilla filling crowned with chocolate. These bars—with a coconut pecan crust, vanilla cream cheese filling, and dark chocolate ganache—are for people who like the idea of the Nanaimo bar but wish it were different: less sweet, more grown-up, a bit modern. Oh, and these are baked. Thus, no claims to authenticity . . . only a very good bar created by a very good friend, Portland food maven Maya Klein.

INGREDIENTS

1½ CUPS (5 OUNCES) CHOCOLATE COOKIE CRUMBS (FROM 9 CHOCOLATE GRAHAM CRACKERS)

½ CUP (1.5 OUNCES) UNSWEETENED DRIED SHREDDED COCONUT

½ CUP (2 OUNCES) FINELY CHOPPED PECANS

8 TABLESPOONS (1 STICK) UNSALTED BUTTER, MELTED

½ CUP PLUS 2 TABLESPOONS (4.375 OUNCES) GRANULATED SUGAR

8 OUNCES CREAM CHEESE, AT ROOM TEMPERATURE

2 TABLESPOONS (0.875 OUNCE) PACKED BROWN SUGAR

½ TEASPOON PURE VANILLA EXTRACT

1 LARGE EGG

½ CUP HEAVY CREAM

7 OUNCES SEMISWEET OR BITTERSWEET CHOCOLATE WITH 55% TO 60% CACAO

EQUIPMENT

9-INCH SQUARE METAL BAKING PAN, THE BOTTOM AND ALL 4 SIDES LINED WITH FOIL (SEE PAGE 19)

Preheat the oven to 350°F. Position a rack in the lower third of the oven.

Mix the crumbs, coconut, pecans, butter, and ¼ cup of the granulated sugar and pat it very firmly into the lined pan. Bake the crust for 10 to 12 minutes or until it looks slightly darker at the edges and smells toasted.

While the crust is baking, mix the filling. In a large bowl, beat the softened cream cheese, brown sugar, and ¼ cup of the remaining granulated sugar until smooth. Beat in the vanilla and then the egg. When the crust is baked, dollop the filling onto the hot crust and spread gently with the back of a spoon. Bake the bars until the edges are slightly puffed, about 10 minutes. Cool on a rack for 30 minutes. Chill for at least 2 hours.

Dissolve the remaining 2 tablespoons granulated sugar in the cream. Bring ½ inch of water to a simmer in a medium skillet. Coarsely chop the chocolate and combine with the cream in a medium metal bowl. Place the bowl directly in the skillet of hot water and turn off the heat. Let rest for 5 minutes and whisk until smooth. Set aside until needed.

Pour the warm ganache onto the bars, spread, and chill for at least 30 minutes before serving. Lift the bars out of the pan by using the edges of the foil liner. Cut into 16 or 25 squares, wiping the knife between cuts. The bars may be stored in an airtight container in the refrigerator for 3 to 4 days.

GOOEY TURTLE BARS

For the sweet tooth: salty and sweet, crunchy and creamy all together in one decadent bar. Divine-but-easy-to-make soft vanilla caramel atop a buttery shortbread crust with loads of toasted pecan halves and chocolate shards. Sinful but celebratory. Might as well make a big batch. This shortcut caramel with sweetened condensed milk is fairly foolproof if you follow the directions and use a silicone spatula to keep the sides of the pot clean. Salt fans will want to top these with extra-tiny pinches of flaky salt. Be my guest.

INGREDIENTS

1 RECIPE SHORTBREAD CRUST (PAGE 96)

1¾ CUPS (12.25 OUNCES) PACKED BROWN SUGAR

¼ CUP HONEY OR LIGHT CORN SYRUP

⅜ TEASPOON SALT (½ TEASPOON FOR COARSE OR FLAKY SEA SALT)

¼ CUP WATER

4 TABLESPOONS UNSALTED BUTTER

ONE 14-OUNCE CAN SWEETENED CONDENSED MILK

1 TABLESPOON PURE VANILLA EXTRACT

2 CUPS (7 OUNCES) WHOLE PECAN HALVES, TOASTED (SEE PAGE 14)

6 OUNCES MILK CHOCOLATE OR SEMISWEET CHOCOLATE, COARSELY CHOPPED, OR 1 CUP MILK CHOCOLATE OR SEMISWEET CHOCOLATE CHIPS

EQUIPMENT

9-BY-13-INCH METAL BAKING PAN, THE BOTTOM AND ALL 4 SIDES LINED WITH FOIL (SEE PAGE 19)

SILICONE SPATULA

CANDY THERMOMETER

continued

Preheat the oven to 325°F. Position a rack in the lower third of the oven.

Prepare the shortbread crust as directed.

To make the topping: In a heavy 2- to 3-quart saucepan (about 8 inches in diameter), combine the brown sugar, honey, salt, and water. Set on medium heat and drop in the chunk of butter. Stir constantly with a heatproof spatula, scraping the corners and bottom of the pan as the butter melts. From time to time, scrape the mixture off the spatula against the top edge of the pan and scrape the sides of the pan clean. Bring the mixture to a medium boil and continue stirring and scraping the pan for about 3 minutes, dissolving the sugar. Stir in the condensed milk and return to a boil, stirring constantly, scraping the sides, corners, and bottom of the pan. Adjust the heat so the mixture boils actively but not too furiously. Continue stirring and cooking until the mixture registers 235°F. Total cooking time will be close to 15 minutes. Remove the pan from the heat and stir in the vanilla. Scrape the hot caramel over the warm crust.

Tilt the pan to level the caramel. Scatter the toasted pecans and chopped chocolate over the surface and set aside until the caramel is cool and the chocolate is set.

Lift the ends of the foil liner and transfer to a cutting board. Peel the foil away from the edges on all four sides. Slide a knife or spatula under the crust to detach the foil. Holding the bars in place, slide the foil out from under it. Use a long sharp knife to cut 35 bars. The bars may be kept in an airtight container for at least 1 week.

RESOURCES

Anson Mills
803-467-4122
ansonmills.com

Stone-ground organic whole grains, including whole wheat, buckwheat, and corn.

Bob's Red Mill Natural Foods
800-349-2173
bobsredmill.com

An extraordinary array of stone-ground flours, including whole wheat, graham, kamut, and spelt flours, cornmeal, and much more.

Guittard Chocolate Company
800-468-2462
guittard.com

This venerable fifth-generation family-owned California company makes superb chocolates for cooking and eating as well as excellent Dutch process and natural cocoa powders. Selections include organic, single original, and signature blends—and exquisite milk chocolates too.

India Tree
800-369-4848
indiatree.com

A great resource for spices and muscovado sugar and decorating sugars made with natural colors. Products are available in specialty stores and better supermarkets, but you can also order online.

King Arthur Flour
800-827-6836
kingarthurflour.com

A comprehensive source of ingredients, cookie scoops, and other tools for cookie makers.

Market Hall Foods
5655 College Avenue
Oakland, CA 94618
888-952-4005
rockridgemarkethall.com

A fabulous gourmet store with a second location in Berkeley. The buyers and owners solicit advice from an impressive list of local cookbook authors and professional bakers, so the store has a subspecialty in baking ingredients and chocolate. Chocolate and cocoa from Scharffen Berger, Valrhona, Callebaut, E. Guittard, and Michel Cluizel, among others; Madagascar and Tahitian vanilla extracts and whole and ground vanilla beans; honeys; chestnut flour; nut pastes; flavored salts; specialty sugars; olive oils; preserves; and more.

Penzey's Spices
800-741-7787
penzeys.com

All kinds of spices; Madagascar, Tahitian, and Mexican vanilla beans; several types of cinnamon. Reading the catalog is an education in flavor ingredients and their uses.

Scharffen Berger
Chocolate Maker
866-608-6944
scharffenberger.com

Some of my favorite semisweet, bittersweet, extra-dark, unsweetened, and milk chocolates; limited-edition special chocolate blends; cacao nibs; and the best natural cocoa powder.

Sur La Table
800-243-0852
surlatable.com

A premium source for quality tools and equipment for home bakers and cooks; ingredients including Scharffen Berger, Valrhona, and E. Guittard chocolates.

Whole Foods
512-477-4455
wholefoodsmarket.com

This upscale national natural food chain is a great source of natural and organic ingredients, including specialty flours and sugars; fine chocolates; bulk foods, including seeds, nuts, and grains; unsweetened shredded, dried, and flaked coconut; and more.

INDEX

Note: Page numbers in *italics* refer to illustrations.

CONVERSION CHARTS

Here are rounded-off equivalents between the metric system and the traditional systems that are used in the United States to measure weight and volume.

FRACTIONS	DECIMALS
⅛	.125
¼	.25
⅓	.33
⅜	.375
½	.5
⅝	.625
⅔	.67
¾	.75
⅞	.875

WEIGHTS

US/UK	METRIC
¼ oz	7 g
½ oz	15 g
1 oz	30 g
2 oz	55 g
3 oz	85 g
4 oz	110 g
5 oz	140 g
6 oz	170 g
7 oz	200 g
8 oz (½ lb)	225 g
9 oz	250 g
10 oz	280 g
11 oz	310 g
12 oz	340 g
13 oz	370 g
14 oz	400 g
15 oz	425 g
16 oz (1 lb)	455 g

VOLUME

AMERICAN	IMPERIAL	METRIC
¼ tsp		1.25 ml
½ tsp		2.5 ml
1 tsp		5 ml
½ Tbsp (1½ tsp)		7.5 ml
1 Tbsp (3 tsp)		15 ml
¼ cup (4 Tbsp)	2 fl oz	60 ml
⅓ cup (5 Tbsp)	2½ fl oz	75 ml
½ cup (8 Tbsp)	4 fl oz	125 ml
⅔ cup (10 Tbsp)	5 fl oz	150 ml
¾ cup (12 Tbsp)	6 fl oz	175 ml
1 cup (16 Tbsp)	8 fl oz	250 ml
1¼ cups	10 fl oz	300 ml
1½ cups	12 fl oz	350 ml
2 cups (1 pint)	16 fl oz	500 ml
2½ cups	20 fl oz (1 pint)	625 ml
5 cups	40 fl oz (1 qt)	1.25 l

OVEN TEMPERATURES

	°F	°C	GAS MARK
very cool	250–275	130–140	½–1
cool	300	148	2
warm	325	163	3
moderate	350	177	4
moderately hot	375–400	190–204	5–6
hot	425	218	7
very hot	450–475	232–245	8–9

°C/F TO °F/C CONVERSION CHART

°C/F	°C	°F	°C/F	°C	°F	°C/F	°C	°F	°C/F	°C	°F
90	32	194	220	104	428	350	177	662	480	249	896
100	38	212	230	110	446	360	182	680	490	254	914
110	43	230	240	116	464	370	188	698	500	260	932
120	49	248	250	121	482	380	193	716	510	266	950
130	54	266	260	127	500	390	199	734	520	271	968
140	60	284	270	132	518	400	204	752	530	277	986
150	66	302	280	138	536	410	210	770	540	282	1,004
160	71	320	290	143	554	420	216	788	550	288	1,022
170	77	338	300	149	572	430	221	806			
180	82	356	310	154	590	440	227	824			
190	88	374	320	160	608	450	232	842			
200	93	392	330	166	626	460	238	860			
210	99	410	340	171	644	470	243	878			

Example: If your temperature is 90°F, your conversion is 32°C; if your temperature is 90°C, your conversion is 194°F.

Library of Congress Cataloging-in-Publication Data

Names: Medrich, Alice, author.
Title: The artisanal kitchen. Holiday cookies / Alice Medrich.
Other titles : Holiday cookies
Description: New York, NY : Artisan, a division of Workman Publishing Co., Inc. [2017] | Includes index.
Identifiers: LCCN 2017005079 | ISBN 9781579658045 (paper-over-board)
Subjects: LCSH: Cookies. | Holiday cooking. | LCGFT: Cookbooks.
Classification: LCC TX772 .M432165 2017 | DDC 641.86/54—dc23 LC record available at https://lccn.loc.gov/2017005079

Cover design by Erica Heitman-Ford

Cover photographs by Lauren Volo (front cover and back cover, left and center) and Deborah Jones (back cover, right)

Design by Erica Heitman-Ford

Artisan books are available at special discounts when purchased in bulk for premiums and sales promotions as well as for fund-raising or educational use. Special editions or book excerpts also can be created to specification. For details, contact the Special Sales Director at the address below, or send an e-mail to specialmarkets@workman.com.

For speaking engagements, contact speakersbureau@workman.com.

Published by Artisan
A division of Workman Publishing Co., Inc.
225 Varick Street
New York, NY 10014-4381
artisanbooks.com

Artisan is a registered trademark of Workman Publishing Co., Inc.

This book has been adapted from *Chewy Gooey Crispy Crunchy Melt-in-Your-Mouth Cookies* by Alice Medrich (Artisan, 2010) and *Seriously Bitter Sweet* (Artisan, 2013).

Published simultaneously in Canada by Thomas Allen & Son, Limited

Printed in China

10 9 8 7 6 5 4 3